Murder for the Asking

A Play

Derek Benfield

Samuel French – London
New York – Sydney – Toronto – Hollywood

Copyright © 1967 by Derek Benfield
All Rights Reserved

MURDER FOR THE ASKING is fully protected under the copyright laws of the British Commonwealth, including Canada, the United States of America, and all other countries of the Copyright Union. All rights, including professional and amateur stage productions, recitation, lecturing, public reading, motion picture, radio broadcasting, television and the rights of translation into foreign languages are strictly reserved.

ISBN 978-0-573-11293-5

www.samuelfrench.co.uk
www.samuelfrench.com

FOR AMATEUR PRODUCTION ENQUIRIES

UNITED KINGDOM AND WORLD EXCLUDING NORTH AMERICA

plays@samuelfrench.co.uk
020 7255 4302/01

Each title is subject to availability from Samuel French, depending upon country of performance.

CAUTION: Professional and amateur producers are hereby warned that MURDER FOR THE ASKING is subject to a licensing fee. Publication of this play does not imply availability for performance. Both amateurs and professionals considering a production are strongly advised to apply to the appropriate agent before starting rehearsals, advertising, or booking a theatre. A licensing fee must be paid whether the title is presented for charity or gain and whether or not admission is charged.

The professional rights in this play are controlled by The Agency (London) Ltd, 24 Pottery Lane, Holland Park, London W11 4 LZ.

No one shall make any changes in this title for the purpose of production. No part of this book may be reproduced, stored in a retrieval system, or transmitted in any form, by any means, now known or yet to be invented, including mechanical, electronic, photocopying, recording, videotaping, or otherwise, without the prior written permission of the publisher. No one shall upload this title, or part of this title, to any social media websites.

The right of Derek Benfield to be identified as author of this work has been asserted in accordance with Section 77 of the Copyright, Designs and Patents Act 1988.

MURDER FOR THE ASKING

This play was first presented by Richard Burnett at the De La Warr Pavilion, Bexhill-on-Sea. It was subsequently presented by Folk Theatre, Ltd. on a national tour which opened at the New Theatre, Hull, on November 14th, 1966, with the following cast:

HENRY SCRUBB	*Eric Lander*
DORA SCRUBB	*Maureen O'Reilly*
JANET GREGORY	*Alison Frazer*
JAMES FRANKLYN	*Stuart Saunders*
DETECTIVE-SERGEANT THATCHER	*Frederick Jaeger*
FRED PENDER	*Kenneth Seeger*
RITA FRANKLYN	*Lyn Hooker*

Directed by FREDERICK JAEGER

Setting by SUSAN AYRES

The play takes place in the furnished ground floor flat of a converted house in the suburbs of a big city. The time is the present.

ACT ONE	Scene 1	Friday evening
	Scene 2	Saturday morning
ACT TWO		A few seconds later
ACT THREE	Scene 1	Saturday evening
	Scene 2	An hour later

No character in this play is intended to portray any specific person, alive or dead.

The running time of this play, excluding intervals, is approximately one hour and fifty minutes.

Other plays by Derek Benfield:

Beyond a Joke
A Bird in the Hand
Caught on the Hop
Fish Out of Water (original version)
Fish Out of Water (revised version)
Flying Feathers
In for the Kill
Look Who's Talking
Off the Hook
Panic Stations
Post Horn Gallop
Running Riot
Touch and Go
Wild Goose Chase

ACT I   Scene I

The furnished, ground-floor flat of a converted house in the suburbs of a big city. There is a kitchenette with a large window stage right, and the door leading to the hall is U.C. Another door U.L. leads to the bedroom and there is a gas fire with a meter D.L. The hall outside the flat door leads off L. to the front door and off R. to the stairs and other flats. There is an armchair L.C. and a smaller chair below the fire. A sofa stands C. at a slight angle towards the fire, and R.C. is a table with three dining chairs. There is another chair against the wall D.R. and a sideboard L. of the door.

The flat is inexpensively but attractively furnished. Though there is obviously little money about, DORA *has managed to keep the place reasonably cheerful with pleasant curtains, cushion covers, etc., and she is clearly a woman of some ingenuity.*

        HENRY SCRUBB, *a pleasant, somewhat pathetic man of about 40, is asleep in the armchair. An open newspaper has fallen to the floor beside him and the radio is playing quietly.*

        After a moment the front door-bell rings. He does not react. It rings again. He stirs, blinks sleepily, stretches and yawns. He rises and goes to peer at the clock on the mantelpiece. It is later than he thought.

HENRY Oh, blimey!
        (He quickly picks up the newspaper and turns off the radio. The doorbell rings again.)
        All right! All right! I'm coming!
        (He goes out to the front door.)
        (off) Oh, it's you.
        (DORA SCRUBB *comes in. She wears a head scarf and a raincoat, and carries a bag of groceries and a paper bag containing a jumper. He follows her in.)*
        I wondered who it was.

DORA Who were you expecting? The Queen Mother?
        (She puts down the groceries on the table and starts to take off her raincoat.)

Don't think I've been off my feet all day. Talk about rush And you never saw such a queue at the 'bus. That's why I'm a bit late. Hope you weren't worried.

HENRY H'm?

DORA Worried. I said I hope you weren't worried.

HENRY Oh. No—no, I wasn't worried, luv.

DORA (*arriving at the fireplace*) Oh, *there's* my key. On the mantelpiece all the time. Knew I'd left it somewhere. (*She puts the key into her handbag*) You were a long time answering the bell. (*She puts her handbag on the armchair.*)

HENRY Was I?

DORA I rang for ages.

HENRY Yes, well I—I was on the top of the steps.

DORA What on earth were you doing up there?

HENRY Cleaning. The shelves. Needed cleaning—you know.

DORA (*crossing to him*) Oh, that was nice of you, Henry. And all the time I was ringing the bell I was saying to myself, 'I bet the old devil's asleep!' (*She gives him a little kiss.*)

HENRY (*laying it on*) I've had quite a busy day, I can tell you. I cleaned all in here, too.

DORA Yes, Henry. I can see you did. (*She picks up some rubbish from the floor and throws it into the waste basket.*)

HENRY I must have missed that bit. (*He puts his newspaper under one of the sofa cushions.*)

(*She smiles and takes her coat into the bedroom.*)

DORA (*off*) It won't be a very exciting supper to-night, I'm afraid. I didn't have much time at lunch. (*Returning.*) Cheese on toast be all right?

HENRY Don't worry about me. I'm—I'm not very hungry.

DORA What? Not after all that hard work, dear?
(*She crosses to the kitchenette.*)

HENRY Why don't we have something later on—you know—before we go to bed?

DORA Well, if you're not hungry, I am.

HENRY I tell you what—you go out to the café down the road. Get yourself a good meal.

DORA Cheese on toast'll do me. (*She busies herself sorting out groceries at the kitchenette.*) Did you pay the milkman?

HENRY The milkman?

DORA I asked you to pay him.

HENRY (*moving to the fireplace*) Er—well, no. No, I didn't.

SCENE I   MURDER FOR THE ASKING

DORA   Oh, Henry! I wish you'd remember sometimes.
HENRY   I didn't have enough money.
DORA   What are you talking about? I left you seven-and-six.
HENRY   Yes. I know you did, dear, but——
     (DORA *moves back from the kitchenette to R. of the sofa.*)
DORA   You didn't spend it, did you?
HENRY   No, of course I didn't! Well, not *all* of it. But you see, there was Sam and Charlie down the local at dinner time so I had to buy them one, didn't I?
DORA   Why?
HENRY   H'm?
DORA   Why did you have to buy them one? They couldn't pay for their own, I suppose? Not likely! Do they know you're out of work?
HENRY   No, I—I don't think so. We didn't talk about it.
DORA   Too proud to tell them, I suppose?
HENRY   It wasn't that. It just never come up, that's all. It never come up.
     (*She returns to the kitchenette.*)
DORA   Why you had to go to the pub at all I don't know.
HENRY   (*sulking a little*) Thought I might hear something.
DORA   Oh, yes—that's likely!
HENRY   It happens sometimes! You mix around and you hear of something.
DORA   How, if nobody knows you're looking for work?
HENRY   I could still hear.
DORA   All you'd hear from Charlie is about Charlie. And as for Sam Egerton, he never opens his mouth except to say 'Another pint, please'.
HENRY   That's not true, Dora. (*He sits on the sofa.*)
DORA   You'd have been better off down the reading room at the library, looking through the 'Wanted' ads.
HENRY   I looked this morning.
     (*She gives him a doubtful look.*)
DORA   Really?
HENRY   I did! Looked through the lot. Nothing doing.
     (*She gets the evening papers from the carrier bag and brings them to him.*)
DORA   Well, I've brought the evening papers. Here you are. Better have a go at them. (*She starts to go but stops as he speaks.*)

HENRY Dora——
DORA Well?
HENRY (*quietly*) I am trying, you know.
(*She looks at him for a moment, smiles, pats his hand affectionately.*)
DORA Yes. Yes, Henry. I know you are.
HENRY Just out of luck. You know how it is. Out of luck, that's all. But I'll have a job soon. You see.
DORA Yes, Henry. Of course you will. I'm sorry.
HENRY I don't enjoy the thought of you having to go out to work every day. It's not what I want for you.
DORA I know, love. I know.
HENRY It'll change. You see. Things'll all change.
(*There is a moment between them, then* DORA *breaks it and moves away. He starts to look through the papers.*)
DORA Well, I mustn't stand here talking to you all night or we'll get no supper at all. (*She starts to lay the table.*)
HENRY I'm really not hungry, love—and I would like you to go out and have a decent meal. (*He crosses to the fireplace.*)
DORA You trying to get rid of me?
HENRY Now why should I want to do a thing like that?
DORA Well, you're very keen on me going out all of a sudden.
HENRY I'm only thinking of you. I mean, where did you go for your lunch to-day?
HENRY The A.B.C. of course. Tomato soup and a buttered roll.
DORA There you are, you see. You ought to have a proper meal.
HENRY Anything doing?
DORA (*studying the newspaper*) No. Same old stuff. You need qualifications for these. No qualifications, that's my trouble.
DORA What about that job you had at the post office? That didn't need no qualifications.
HENRY That was at Christmas time. They don't need anybody now. Tomato soup's not enough to keep you going this cold weather.
DORA Well, it'll have to do for the time being.
(*There is a tap at the door.*)
Come in.
(*The door opens and* JANET GREGORY *comes in. She is a cheerful, blonde Cockney typist of about 20.*)
JANET Here! You're a bit late to-night, Dora.

SCENE I   MURDER FOR THE ASKING

DORA Oh, hullo, Janet.
JANET I'd just about given you up. Then I heard the front door so I finished my supper and came straight down.
HENRY Yes, you would!
JANET Dear me! You sound a bit surly to-night, darling.
HENRY Well, what did you have to come down for?
JANET Only being friendly.
HENRY Oh, is *that* what it was?
JANET (*mock disappointed*) Oh, aren't you pleased to see me, Lover Boy? (*She gives him a look and turns to* DORA.) Here, Dora, you remember that feller I told you about last night?
DORA Six foot two from the Bank of England?
JANET No. Five foot ten from Marks and Spencer's.
DORA Oh, yes. I remember.
JANET He asked me, to-day! We're going to the pictures Sunday night. He's ever so good-looking. Not glamorous, mind you. More the rugged type—you know.
HENRY (*wearily*) Is *that* all you came down to tell us?
JANET I thought you'd be pleased. Take my mind off you.
HENRY Janet, if you don't mind—we are rather busy.
JANET Oh? Well, that makes a change, doesn't it? (*To* DORA.) What's got into him to-night? Bit edgy, isn't he?
DORA He's all right. Oh, before I forget—I got your jumper from the cleaners at lunchtime. (*She goes to get it.*)
JANET Good. I hoped you'd remember.
DORA It's come up quite well, I think.
   (JANET *takes the jumper out of the paper bag and holds it up in front of her.*)
JANET Let's have a look. Yes, that's lovely! (*She turns to* HENRY.) I'll look fab in that on Sunday, won't I, Henry? (*She sees his blank look.*) Oh, well, never mind. I know you'd like me to stay here but I think I'd better tear myself away. (*She turns at the door.*) Goodbye, darling! (HENRY *turns away.* JANET *grins at* DORA *and goes out quickly.*)
DORA Did you *have* to say that to her?
HENRY Eh?
DORA You *were* a bit rude, you know. Are you feeling all right?
HENRY 'Course I'm all right. She's always popping in and out of here. I just get a bit sick of it sometimes, that's all. (*He turns away.*)

(DORA *looks at him thoughtfully for a moment, then shrugs it off and goes back to the laying of the table. There is a short pause.*)

DORA You never heard any more, then?

HENRY Eh?

DORA From that letter you wrote. The box number, don't you remember? That one said no qualifications, didn't it?

HENRY Oh, yes. I'd forgotten about that.

DORA 'Big financial reward'—isn't that what it said?

HENRY Oh, I'd have heard by now.

DORA You never know. You did post the letter, didn't you?

HENRY 'Course I posted it! I told you it was no good at the time. Forget about it, Dora.
(*There is a slight pause. He moves towards her a little.*)
You know what I think? There's only one thing for us to do.

DORA And what's that?

HENRY Move away from here. Pack up and move away. Start afresh—you know.
(*She moves to above the sofa.*)

DORA (*wearily*) And where would we go to?

HENRY Well—anywhere. Just another place where we can begin again.

DORA You think it would be any different?

HENRY Why not? It's worth a try, Dora. A new place. Your luck can change in a new place. Besides, I—I *want* to go. (*He sinks on to the sofa.*)

DORA Why?

HENRY I've had enough of it here. Sick of it, I am. Sick of it. Anyway, how much longer do you think we can afford the rent of this place?
(*She looks at him for a moment, then she moves around to sit beside him comfortingly.*)

DORA It'll be all right, Henry. When things get better it'll be all right. You'll see. You're bound to feel fed up and depressed now, but we can't run away just because we're down on our luck.

HENRY I'm not running away, Dora. I just don't see the point of staying here with things as they are.

DORA What about *my* job? At least *I've* got a job here.

HENRY And how do you think I feel about that?

DORA There's no need.
(*He rises and moves to the fireplace.*)
HENRY No, Dora. I've made up my mind. After to-night we're moving.
DORA After to-night? What's so special about to-night?
HENRY I only meant after to-night we'll really make plans—you know.
DORA (*with a smile*) You're a funny man.
HENRY Oh, yes! (*Returning to her.*) Here—I've got an idea! Why don't you go down and see that film, eh? The one you said you'd like to see.
DORA Here you go again!
HENRY Well, you deserve a break, Dora. Go to the pictures and bring back some fish and chips afterwards! What do you say?
DORA I say you've gone mad.
HENRY Please, Dora—I'd like you to.
DORA Now, Henry, be sensible—I'm not going to spend money we can't afford.
HENRY Borrow some of the rent money.
DORA And when the time comes to pay the rent? What then?
HENRY We'll think of something. Something'll turn up. You'd enjoy it. Take you out of yourself a bit. After all, you go out to work every day, you're entitled to a bit of pleasure, aren't you?
DORA (*weakening*) Oh, Henry! No—it wouldn't be right.
HENRY Who cares? It wouldn't cost much. We could save a bit on the gas the next few weeks. We'll do it somehow. Come on! Why not? I could do with some fish and chips.
(*She looks at him for a moment, makes up her mind.*)
DORA All right, Henry—I will!
HENRY That's my girl! Go and get your coat. (*He urges her towards the bedroom door.*)
DORA What—now?
HENRY Yes. The film starts in half an hour.
DORA How do *you* know?
HENRY I—I saw the times when I was passing.
DORA You planned this, didn't you?
HENRY Why not? Go on—get off with you!

(She laughs and goes out to the bedroom. He starts to look towards the sofa as she returns.)

DORA What about you? Why don't you come with me?

HENRY You know I hate the pictures. Besides, I—I want to see to that shelf. It needs fixing.

DORA All right, love. *(She goes off into the bedroom again.)*

(He looks after her to make sure she has gone, then he goes quickly to her handbag, opens it and takes out the latch-key. He puts it in his trouser pocket and replaces the handbag as she returns with her coat on.)

Are you sure you don't mind?

HENRY 'Course I don't! You go on.

(She collects her handbag.)

DORA I don't know what's come over you, I'm sure!

HENRY I just want you to enjoy yourself, that's all.

DORA All right, then. I'll see you later. Goodbye, luv. *(She kisses him briefly and goes to the door.)* Here—you're not up to something, are you?

HENRY Now what would I be up to?

(She smiles at him fondly and goes out. HENRY *remains still for a moment until he hears the front door slam, then he opens the flat door and looks out quickly to make sure she has gone. Satisfied he returns and closes the door and with a certain sense of urgency begins to tidy away a few things —groceries, newspapers, etc.—and folds up and puts away the tablecloth. He slightly re-arranges the furniture in an attempt to make it look more presentable, then he goes to the mirror over the fireplace and fastens up his shirt collar, realises he has no tie and goes off to the bedroom to get one. He returns and ties the tie, then he collects his jacket from the chair D.R. and puts it on. He smoothes his hair back with his hands and is then apparently satisfied with his appearance. On an impulse he crosses to the kitchenette and gets out a bottle of beer. He opens it and pours the beer into a glass. He is about to drink it when the front door bell goes. He puts down the glass and the bottle on the table and starts for the door, then he returns quickly to drink some of the beer. He then goes out to the front door.*

We hear the mutter of voices, and then HENRY *returns followed by* JAMES FRANKLYN. HENRY *closes the door*

SCENE I   MURDER FOR THE ASKING   13

of the flat as FRANKLYN moves down into the room. FRANKLYN is a well-dressed, distinguished-looking man of about 55.)

FRANKLYN (glancing at his watch) Seven-thirty. Right on the dot. You did well.
HENRY I thought she wasn't going to go, at first. Didn't seem at all keen.
FRANKLYN That's the trouble with women. They're so unpredictable.
HENRY Er—won't you sit down, Mr. Franklyn?
FRANKLYN Thank you. (He sits in the armchair.) How long will she be gone?
HENRY About two hours at least. She's gone to the pictures.
FRANKLYN She won't change her mind and turn back?
HENRY She'll have to ring the front door bell if she does. I took her latchkey. (He holds it up for FRANKLYN to see.)
(FRANKLYN smiles in admiration.)
FRANKLYN Good.
(HENRY puts the latchkey in his jacket pocket.)
Then we have plenty of time.
HENRY Yes. Yes, that's right.
FRANKLYN (looking about) H'm. Quite nice. Not nearly so bad as your letter led me to believe.
HENRY We shan't be able to afford this much longer, I can tell you. If things haven't changed by the end of the month we'll be out of here. I've had a rough time lately.
FRANKLYN We must change that, then—mustn't we?
(HENRY holds FRANKLYN's look for a moment, then moves away.)
HENRY Would you like a glass of beer? I think I've got a—
FRANKLYN No, thank you, Mr. Scrubb. (With a smile.) Why don't you sit down?
HENRY Oh—er—yes. Yes. (He sits on the sofa.)
FRANKLYN I expect you think this is all very mysterious?
HENRY Well, it is a bit unusual, isn't it?
FRANKLYN Yes.
(FRANKLYN holds HENRY's look for a moment, then rises and moves about as if making an appraisal of the house.)
How many other people live in the house, Mr. Scrubb?
HENRY Oh, there are two flats above this. Then there are—let me see—three bed-sits on the top floor.
FRANKLYN All occupied?

HENRY   No. There's one vacant at the moment.
          (FRANKLYN *crosses slowly behind the sofa to R. of* HENRY.)
FRANKLYN   And the basement?
HENRY   There's a young couple down there. Moved in about a year ago.
FRANKLYN   I see. Have you any particular friends in the house?
HENRY   Oh, no. Just to pass the time of day, that's all.
FRANKLYN   But no one who would be likely to know the details of your life, your routine? No one who would notice any-thing—unusual?
HENRY   Only the girl, Janet.
FRANKLYN   H'm?
HENRY   Janet Gregory. She lives in one of the flats above this. She never misses much. (*Pause.*) Does it matter? Whether people know about me, I mean?
FRANKLYN   It might.
HENRY   (*with sudden impatience*) Look, you didn't *have* to come here, you know!
FRANKLYN   Didn't I, Mr. Scrubb? *Didn't* I?
HENRY   (*weakening again*) Well—I mean—I could have come to see *you* about the job quite easily.
FRANKLYN   Yes, I know. But, you see, it was better this way. You'll understand why presently.
          (HENRY *shifts uncomfortably under* FRANKLYN's *steady, appraising gaze.*)
HENRY   Are you sure you won't have that beer?
FRANKLYN   Quite sure, thank you.
HENRY   (*rising*) Well—a cigarette? I think I've got——
FRANKLYN   No, thank you. (*He produces a cigar from a case in his pocket.*) I prefer these. Will you have one?
HENRY   No, thanks.
          (HENRY *fetches a box of matches from the mantelpiece, strikes one and holds it out to* FRANKLYN. FRANKLYN *lights his cigar, watching* HENRY's *hand which is shaking slightly.*)
FRANKLYN   Are you nervous, Mr. Scrubb?
HENRY   No, no! I had a few beers at lunch time—you know——
FRANKLYN   You wouldn't say that you were a nervous type of man?
HENRY   Oh, no. Not nervous—no.
FRANKLYN   Good. (*Crossing to the fireplace.*) I mean, it wouldn't do to be nervous, you know. A nervous man is an unreliable

SCENE I MURDER FOR THE ASKING 15

     man. And an unreliable man is a useless man. Are you a reliable man, Mr. Scrubb?
HENRY Well, yes—yes, I think so.
FRANKLYN You're quite sure you want to go through with this?
HENRY What do you mean? Of course I do!
FRANKLYN If you didn't want to go through with it you should never have invited me here.
HENRY I don't know what you're getting at.
FRANKLYN Don't you, Mr. Scrubb?
     (*There is a pause.* HENRY *puts the spent match in the ashtray on the table. He is bewildered and beginning to be a little afraid.* FRANKLYN *resumes his seat.*)
     How long have you lived here?
HENRY (*puzzled*) About two years. I was saying to Dora to-night—it's time we went away. I want to get away from here.
FRANKLYN Oh, you mustn't do that. Not yet. Not until—after it's all over.
HENRY After *what's* all over?
     (*But* FRANKLYN *does not enlarge.*)
FRANKLYN I liked your letter. It was a frank, honest letter. And now that I meet you I see that you are indeed a frank, honest sort of man. What sort of a job had you in mind?
HENRY (*moving to* R. *of* FRANKLYN) Anything! Anything at all. I'm pretty desperate. If something doesn't turn up soon I don't know what I'm going to do.
FRANKLYN So we can say then that you aren't too particular about the type of work?
HENRY No. Anything that I can do. (*With a faint attempt at bravado.*) As long as the money's all right.
FRANKLYN (*with a smile*) Oh, I think I can promise you that the money will be all right, Mr. Scrubb.
     (HENRY, *puzzled, moves to below the sofa.*)
HENRY Why did you want my wife out of the way? I mean, why shouldn't she know about the job? She's bound to find out. If I get the job she's bound to know.
FRANKLYN But that's precisely what I don't want her to do.
HENRY Not know? Dora not know about the job? She'd be the first person I'd tell!
     (FRANKLYN *rises.*)
FRANKLYN Then in that case there's no point in our talking any further. (*He makes for the door.*)

HENRY Here—wait a minute! What are you getting at? Is this something—secret? Something I mustn't talk about?
FRANKLYN Precisely.
HENRY Well, I dunno—
(*There is a pause.* FRANKLYN, *at the door, watches* HENRY *for a moment.*)
FRANKLYN Well—do we talk? Or do we say goodnight?
(HENRY *is undecided for a moment.*)
HENRY Let's talk.
FRANKLYN Good!
(*He indicates the sofa and* HENRY *nervously resumes his seat.*)
I had quite a few replies to my advertisement, you know.
HENRY Yes. I'm sure you did.
FRANKLYN But I selected the people I wished to interview very carefully and put their names and addresses on my 'short list'. (*He takes out a sheet of paper.*) Here it is, you see. Only three of you. So you're well in the running. (*He puts the list back into his pocket.*)
HENRY I see.
(*An unaccountable atmosphere has crept into the conversation, and* HENRY *is starting to feel apprehensive and nervous.*
FRANKLYN *moves nearer to* HENRY, *looking down at him.*)
FRANKLYN To look at me, Mr Scrubb, would you say that I was a very strong man?
(HENRY *looks up at him, bewildered.*)
HENRY A strong man? Well, I—I don't know. You're a well built man. I *suppose* you're strong.
FRANKLYN I'm not a strong man at all.
HENRY Oh?
FRANKLYN No. I'm anything *but* a strong man.
(*There is a moment's silence, then there is a sudden knock at the door. They react.* HENRY *rises to R. of the sofa.*)
(*softly*) Who the hell's that?
HENRY I dunno.
FRANKLYN You're not expecting anyone, are you?
HENRY No—I told you.
FRANKLYN Don't answer it. They'll probably go away if you don't answer it.

(*A pause as they wait. Then there is another knock. Again they wait, anxiously. Again there is a knock, more impatient this time.*)
HENRY (*helplessly*) I shall have to.
FRANKLYN (*after a pause*) All right. Go on. But whoever it is—get rid of them. (*He moves upstage out of the immediate eye-line from the door.*)
(HENRY *goes to the door, turns to look again at* FRANKLYN, *who indicates to open it. He does so.* JANET *is there.*)
JANET What are you doing in there, you naughty old thing? Having a seance or something? I thought you'd never open the door.
HENRY Look, Janet, I'm afraid I'm——
(*But she sails past him into the room, talking as she goes.*)
JANET All right, darling. Don't panic. I won't keep you a second, but I never gave Dora the money for the jumper.
(*She stops as she comes face to face with* FRANKLYN.) Oh. Oh, sorry. I didn't know you had company.
HENRY (*ineffectually*) Er—this is—Mr.—er——
FRANKLYN Brandon.
HENRY But I thought——
FRANKLYN Geoffrey Brandon.
(HENRY, *puzzled, turns to* JANET.)
HENRY This is Janet Gregory. The one I told you about.
FRANKLYN I see. How do you do.
JANET How do you do. (*She eyes him appreciatively.*)
HENRY Mr.—(*Pause.*)—Brandon's selling insurance.
JANET Insurance, eh? How lovely! (*To* FRANKLYN.) I'm a typist.
FRANKLYN That must be very nice.
JANET I suppose *you* don't want a typist, do you?
FRANKLYN Er—no, I'm afraid not.
JANET Pity.
HENRY Dora's out at the moment.
JANET (*turning on him*) Well, I can see that, darling.
HENRY Gone to the pictures.
JANET To the pictures? Not like her. Whatever's come over her? Well—sorry to interrupt. Tell her I looked in.
HENRY Yes. I will.
JANET Ta-ra, then! 'Bye, Mr. Brandon. Nice to have met you.
FRANKLYN It was my pleasure.
JANET Oo! Granted, I'm sure!

(*She goes out.* HENRY *closes the door and moves down into the room.*)

HENRY Sorry about that.

FRANKLYN It wasn't your fault, Mr. Scrubb. Are any of the other inhabitants liable to pop in like that?

HENRY Oh, no. The people in the other flats keep to themselves a bit more.

FRANKLYN I'm very relieved to hear it. (*He resumes his seat.*) Well, now that the ebullient Miss Gregory has gone, let's get down to business, as no doubt she will be waiting to hear me leave as soon as you have said you cannot afford any insurance! What sort of salary had you in mind?

HENRY (*puzzled*) Salary?

FRANKLYN You are presumably interested in the money?

HENRY Yes, of course. It's just that—well, you'd know more about that than me. I mean—it depends on the job, don't it?

FRANKLYN It does indeed. And as far as I know there's no union rate for the job in this case. Would a single payment of three thousand pounds be of any interest to you?

HENRY (*staggered*) Three thousand pounds?

FRANKLYN How long would it take you normally to earn as much as that, Mr. Scrubb? Quite a long time, eh? You can earn three thousand pounds for one evening's work.

HENRY I—I don't follow.

FRANKLYN The job I have to offer is not a permanent post. I require your services for one evening only.

(HENRY *moves quickly to* FRANKLYN.)

HENRY Here! You don't want me to rob a bank, do you?

FRANKLYN No, no! I assure you—it's nothing like that.

HENRY I wouldn't rob a bank if I was——

FRANKLYN I promise you that is not what I had in mind.

HENRY Then what *do* I have to do for the money?

(FRANKLYN *looks up at* HENRY.)

FRANKLYN I want you to kill somebody.

(HENRY *looks at him for a moment, stunned, then he makes abruptly for the door.*)

HENRY You'd better go, mate. Try the next name on your bloody list!

FRANKLYN But you haven't heard the whole of my proposition—

HENRY I've heard enough! Look, I may be badly off, but I'm not going to kill anyone!

SCENE I MURDER FOR THE ASKING 19

FRANKLYN Not even if your victim can be guaranteed not to resist?
HENRY You're barmy! I'm not a ruddy murderer! You must be round the bend! Come on—you get out of here!
(But FRANKLYN *calmly remains seated.*)
FRANKLYN Think what you could do with three thousand pounds.
HENRY Three thousand pounds'd be no good to me in prison, mate! Come on!
FRANKLYN You haven't even asked me who the proposed victim is yet.
HENRY No, and I'm not going to, either. I don't want to know, see? Now you just get out of here before I call a copper.
FRANKLYN Really, Mr. Scrubb, how vehement you have become. And I thought you were such a quiet little man.
HENRY Are you going to get out of here?
FRANKLYN Not until you've heard me out.
HENRY Right! (*He goes and grabs up the bottle from the table.*) You said yourself you weren't a strong man. Well, I'm telling you now—if you aren't out of here in two minutes, I'm going to crown you with this!
(*He stands close to* FRANKLYN, *threatening him with the bottle.* FRANKLYN *looks at him steadily, smiles blandly.*)
FRANKLYN I thought you said you weren't interested in murder.
(HENRY *looks at the bottle in his hand, lowers it and turns away to below the sofa.*)
HENRY (*quietly*) Get out of here. Please get out of here.
(FRANKLYN *rises and crosses to L. of* HENRY.)
FRANKLYN If you really intend to attack me, go ahead. It'll be quite all right with me.
(HENRY *turns to look at him.*)
HENRY What are you up to? What are you trying to make me do?
FRANKLYN I simply want you to hear me out. That's all I ask. Let me at least explain why I came here to see you to-night.
HENRY Look, I don't want to know why you came here to see me. All I wanted was a job, see? Just an ordinary job. I don't want no three thousand pounds. I just want a job—that's all!
FRANKLYN Let me at least tell you who your victim will be. It might make all the difference to you.
HENRY What do you mean? What are you driving at?
FRANKLYN I want you to murder me—please.
(HENRY *is shattered. He backs slowly to the table in horror.*)

HENRY   You're mad. You're stark, staring, raving, bloody mad!
FRANKLYN   On the contrary. Let me explain.
HENRY   I'm not interested, I tell you. For God's sake get out of here!
FRANKLYN   When I told you just now that I wasn't a strong man what I meant was that I have a heart complaint. Apparently rather a serious one. My doctor tells me that I shall be lucky if I live six months.
HENRY   I—I'm sorry.

(FRANKLYN *goes to the mantelpiece to tap the ash from his cigar.*)

FRANKLYN   I wasn't attempting to gain your sympathy. I merely wanted you to understand my situation.
HENRY   Look, I'm sorry about what the doctor told you—but I'm still not a murderer. Now, will you please go?

(FRANKLYN *looks at him for a moment, shakes his head.*)

FRANKLYN   No, Mr. Scrubb. I won't go. If you like to throw me out, then by all means do so. But I will, of course, resist and a rather nasty struggle could ensue. In view of what I have just told you about my heart you might well kill me—by accident—and without the three thousand pounds I have offered you. On the other hand, if you allow me to remain for a few more minutes while I explain, then I give you my word that if your decision is still 'No' I shall walk out of here and will never bother you again.
HENRY   (*after a pause*) I don't seem to have much choice, do I?

(FRANKLYN *moves slowly above the sofa to U.L. of the table as he speaks.*)

FRANKLYN   When I die, Mr. Scrubb—as I apparently shall do within six months—I leave my wife reasonably well off. Nothing more. Not nearly as wealthy as I should have liked.
HENRY   Well, I reckon you're insured, aren't you?
FRANKLYN   Ah, how quickly you come to the crux of the matter! The money realised on my death from life assurance is considerable, but under a clause in the contract this sum will be automatically doubled in the unlikely event of my being murdered. Now, Mr. Scrubb, do you see where *you* come in?
HENRY   No insurance company would pay up.
FRANKLYN   How little you know! After all, the odds against the average citizen being murdered must be considerably greater

than against his not dying at all. So you see my situation. In six months I shall be dead anyway. But if, in the meantime, I am murdered, then my wife will be considerably better provided for. You will be helping my wife, Mr. Scrubb, by doing what I ask.
(HENRY *gazes at him for a moment, dumbfounded.*)

HENRY You *are* mad, aren't you? I won't do it! I'm not a murderer. I couldn't kill anyone—I couldn't!

FRANKLYN Not even to please the victim?

HENRY (*desperately*) Will you please go?

FRANKLYN All right. If that is your decision. I won't go back on my word. Goodnight, Mr. Scrubb. (*He gets to the door and turns.*) Oh—just one thing.

HENRY Well?

FRANKLYN (*taking out a visiting card*) Here is my card. With my telephone number. Just in case you change your mind.

HENRY I won't change my mind.
(FRANKLYN *puts the card on top of the small bookcase near the door and starts to go. He pauses in the doorway.*)

FRANKLYN Three thousand pounds is a very large sum of money. Don't you agree? (*He smiles at* HENRY *and goes out.*)
(*We hear the front door slam.* HENRY *closes the flat door and stands there for a moment. He is in quite a state after the interview. Then he notices the visiting card, takes it up and goes quickly to the wastepaper basket near the fire. He tears up the card and drops the pieces into the basket.*
There is a knock on the door of the flat. HENRY *reacts.*)

HENRY Who is it?
(JANET *opens the door and comes in.*)

JANET (*disappointed*) Oh. Has he gone?

HENRY Yes—just now. (*He moves down to the fireplace.*)

JANET Pity. Look, I'm ever so sorry about barging in like that when you had company. I never thought, you see.

HENRY It's all right. Forget it.

JANET He was a bit of a smasher, wasn't he? You know what I mean? That suit must have set him back a bit.

HENRY I—I didn't notice.

JANET That wasn't off the peg, I can tell you. In insurance, you said?

HENRY (*miles away*) H'm?

JANET That feller who was here. In insurance?
HENRY Oh—yes. Yes, that's right.
JANET Must be doing all right. Quite successful, I'd say.
HENRY Yes.
JANET (*testing the air like a bloodhound*) You been smoking cigars?
HENRY No. No, it was Mr.—Mr. Brandon.
JANET Cigars, eh? Get him! Not quite the usual sort of insurance salesman, eh?
HENRY Was there anything else?
JANET Oh, charming! Aren't you feeling well?
HENRY I'm quite all right. Just a bit tired, that's all.
JANET (*smarting a little*) Well, I had to come and apologise, didn't I?
HENRY Very kind of you.
JANET I'll be off, then. Leave you to it. What time are you expecting Dora back?
HENRY I dunno. Depends on the picture, don't it?
JANET Well, I expect I'll see her in the morning.
HENRY (*wearily*) Yes. I expect you will.
(JANET *turns at the door.*)
JANET Funny time of night for an insurance man to call.
HENRY (*firmly*) Goodnight!
JANET All right—I can take a hint! (*She goes, somewhat put out.*)

> HENRY *loosens his tie and collar, then crosses quickly to finish off the glass of beer which he has left on the table. As he puts down the glass he sees the cigar which* FRANKLYN *has left in the ashtray. He thinks for a moment, then gets a piece of newspaper from under one of the sofa cushions and puts it down on the table. He empties the cigar, ash, etc., from the ashtray on to the paper. He looks about the room, fetches the ashtray from the mantelpiece and empties that on to the newspaper also. He returns the ashtray to the mantelpiece, then crumples up the piece of newspaper and its contents and hides the whole lot at the bottom of the kitchen refuse bin. Relieved, he sits in the armchair, facing R. After a long pause he turns his head slowly and looks towards the wastepaper basket into which he has put the pieces of the visiting card. He reaches out slowly and pulls it a bit nearer. He looks down into*

it thoughtfully, undecided, as the lights FADE to
BLACKOUT.

CURTAIN

ACT I
SCENE II

It is the following morning.

As the CURTAIN *rises* DORA *is in the kitchenette pouring boiling water from the kettle into the tea-pot. She is dressed in her nightdress, dressing gown and slippers. The curtains are open and the gas fire is on. Having made the tea, she puts the tea cosy over the pot and goes to put the tablecloth on the table. She has a sudden thought and goes to look in the oven. With a sigh she takes out a plate of cold fish and chips as the door opens and* HENRY *comes in. He is in his vest, trousers and slippers and is drying his ears with a towel.*

DORA Well! You're a fine one, I must say.
HENRY Eh?
DORA Didn't you want the fish and chips?
HENRY Fish and chips?
DORA Last night. I came back with the fish and chips like you said.
HENRY Oh. Oh, yes. I remember.
DORA Didn't you want them?
HENRY No. I—I made a sandwich earlier. (*He sits on the sofa and starts to change into his shoes.*)
DORA Bit of a waste of money. Buying fish and chips and not eating them.
HENRY Yes.
DORA I mean, I couldn't eat your lot as well as mine. (*She puts the fish and chips down in the kitchenette.*)
HENRY No.
DORA Can't think why you had to go out at that time of night, anyway.
HENRY I had a bit of a headache. I went for a walk. You know—thought the fresh air might clear it.
DORA (*pointedly*) Not much fresh air in the pub.

HENRY I didn't go to the pub.
DORA No? Bit of a long walk then, wasn't it?
HENRY What's wrong with that?
DORA Not like you, that's all. Not like you to go for a long walk at that time of night. I couldn't wait up. I gave you a good half hour then I went to bed.
HENRY Yes. You were fast asleep when I came in.
DORA Ever such a nice picture. A lot of singing. I was glad you made me go. I met old Mr. Thornett from the top floor as I came in.
HENRY Oh, yes? Been out with that dog, I expect.
(DORA *is busy laying the breakfast things.*)
DORA Lucky for me I bumped into him, 'cos I hadn't got my key. Funny thing, you know. I could have sworn I put it in my handbag last night when I found it on the mantelpiece.
HENRY Oh? I don't remember.
DORA But I couldn't find it. Can't find it now. Funny, isn't it?
HENRY Yes, very funny.
(DORA *looks at him for a moment, moves to him.*)
DORA Are you feeling all right, dear?
HENRY Yes—of course.
DORA You're a bit surly this morning.
HENRY Leave me alone, eh?
DORA All that fresh air last night, I expect.
HENRY Oh, lay off, will you?
DORA Pity *you* didn't come to the pictures, too. Might have made you a bit better tempered.
(HENRY *makes for the bedroom.*)
I could warm up that fish for your breakfast.
HENRY No. I'll just have some bread and butter. (*He goes off into the bedroom.*)
(*She watches him go, thoughtfully, then shrugs it off and brings bread, butter, marmalade, etc., to the table.*
There is a knock at the door.)
DORA Come in!
(JANET *looks around the door. She is wearing her coat and hat.*)
JANET Here—where's Lover Boy?
DORA (*with a smile*) He's getting dressed.
JANET Good. (*She closes the door and comes down to* DORA.) Not had your breakfast yet?

SCENE II MURDER FOR THE ASKING

DORA   No. You're off early.
JANET Yes. Off to Sainsbury's. Gets so crowded later on. (*Saucily.*) Here—what about *you* last night? (*She sits above the table.*)
DORA   Me?
JANET Sneaking off to the pictures like that. Must be five or six months since you went off to the pictures. All on your own, too! Why didn't you say you were going when I came down last night? I could have come with you.
DORA   How did you know I'd been to the pictures?
       (*During this,* DORA *is cutting the bread, etc.*)
JANET He told me.
DORA   Henry?
JANET Yes. It was ever so embarrassing! I came down with the money for the jumper, see, not thinking you'd be out. I mean, you're not usually, are you?
DORA   (*laughing*) Well, Henry wouldn't mind. Or did you catch him asleep?
JANET Oh, no! I just thought you'd be in, you know. You might have warned me. I mean—I always try to keep out of the way when you've got visitors.
DORA   Visitors?
JANET He was ever so nice. And well spoken with it.
DORA   Who was?
JANET This feller—this Mr. Brandon. Came face to face with him. I did feel silly! But he was smashing. I wished I could have stayed! (*She laughs saucily.*)
DORA   What time was this?
JANET I suppose it was about half past seven. Perhaps that's why you went out—so they could talk business, eh?
DORA   Er—yes. Yes. That's right.
JANET Lovely suit, he had. Ever such a lovely suit. Expensive—you know. You can tell, can't you? Very expensive suit.
       (HENRY *comes in from the bedroom. He has put on his shirt and cardigan. He sees* JANET.)
HENRY You here again?
JANET (*a little tartly*) I only popped in for a moment. (*To* DORA.) I'll see you later, Dora.
DORA   Yes. 'Bye!
JANET (*to* HENRY) Goodbye, Lover Boy! (*She goes out, closing the door.*)

HENRY She'll be moving her bed in here next.
DORA (*with a smile*) Not if I can help it!
(*We hear the front door slam.*)
Sure you wouldn't like that fish, Henry? It won't take a minute.
HENRY (*patiently*) I don't want the fish, Dora. (*He goes to the table and sits down.*)
DORA I only asked. I don't know what's the matter with you this morning. Bad-tempered and jumpy about everything.
(*She pours the tea. In silence they start breakfast. There is quite a pause.*)
Could have saved yourself one-and-fourpence.
HENRY Eh?
DORA On the fish.
HENRY For God's sake don't keep on about the fish, Dora!
DORA I mean, if I'd known you were going to change your mind I'd only have bought mine.
HENRY Let's drop it, eh? I forgot, that's all. I clean forgot. (*He settles into a piece of bread and butter.*)
DORA Seems a bit daft to forget after all the fuss you made about it. The way you were going on before I went out, you'd have thought I was fetching *smoked* salmon not *rock* salmon. I thought you'd be sitting here waiting with the bread and butter out and the kettle on.
HENRY Well, I wasn't.
DORA No. You were boozing it up down the Bull-and-Royal.
HENRY I told you, Dora—I didn't go to the pub.
(*They eat in silence for a moment.*)
DORA You didn't tell me you had a visitor last night.
HENRY Eh? Oh, yes. She popped in to see you.
DORA I didn't mean Janet.
HENRY Oh? (*As if he had forgotten.*) Oh! You mean when she come in here?
DORA Yes. She said you were talking to someone.
HENRY That's right. He was selling insurance. Canvassing—you know.
DORA Why on earth did you let him in? You know we can't afford it.
HENRY Well, you know what these blokes are like. Give you a lot of chat on the doorstep and in no time at all, they're inside

DORA Marmalade?
HENRY Eh?
DORA With your bread. Marmalade.
HENRY Oh—ta.
(*There is a pause as they get on with their food.*)
DORA Janet was quite taken with him.
HENRY Yes. She would be. Why doesn't she mind her own business? Poking her nose in.
DORA She only said she liked his suit.
HENRY She shouldn't have been in here in the first place!
DORA What does it matter? He was only selling insurance. You make it sound like a dark secret.
HENRY It's you that's doing that!
DORA Me?
HENRY All these questions. Why are you asking all these questions?
DORA (*with a smile*) The way you're going on, anyone'd think Janet had caught you with another woman.
HENRY She's a nosy little devil! I bet she's up there now with her ear pressed to the floor-boards. She knows everything that's going on. Mr. Franklyn had only been gone two minutes and down she came!
DORA Mr. Franklyn?
HENRY This bloke we're talking about!
DORA Janet said his name was Brandon.
HENRY (*after a brief pause*) What the hell does she know about it?
DORA Why should she say his name was Brandon if it wasn't?
HENRY *I* don't know! Maybe—maybe it was Brandon. I don't remember. What does it matter, anyhow?
DORA I didn't say it mattered, Henry. It just seems odd, that's all. (*He gets up abruptly and starts to move away.*)
HENRY All right if I get up? Or have you got some more questions to ask? (*He snatches up the newspaper from the sofa and moves away.*)
DORA There's no need to be like that. You certainly are behaving in a funny way all of a sudden.
HENRY What do you mean?
DORA Well, for a start, last night—the way you wanted me to go out. Practically pushed me out of the door.
HENRY I was only thinking of you——

DORA Then you go off for a walk—late at night. That's a thing you've never done before. You had a visitor and never told me about it——
HENRY I didn't get much chance, did I? Anyhow, I didn't think it was important.
DORA *(enjoying herself)* And whoever the mysterious visitor was he seems to have two names!
HENRY Oh, shut up, will you? *(He sits in the armchair.)*
DORA *(laughing)* Are you *sure* you didn't go into the pub last night?
(The door-bell goes.)
HENRY That our bell?
DORA *(rising)* Yes. It'll be the milkman.
HENRY What's he ringing the bell for?
DORA *(patiently)* He has to be paid sometimes. It is Saturday, you know. *(She gets her bag and fumbles for money. She has not quite enough.)* Have you got a shilling?
HENRY I dunno. Might be one in my jacket pocket.
(She goes to his jacket, which is on the back of the sofa, and looks in the pocket.)
DORA Well I never!
HENRY What is it?
DORA My latchkey! *You* had it all the time.
(She holds out the key which was amongst the small change. They look at each other for a moment.)
HENRY No, luv. That's mine.
DORA It's got my tag on it. Now, what were you doing with my key?
(The door-bell rings again. She goes out to the front door. We hear subdued voices. DORA *returns, followed by a man in a casual overcoat and hat. She leads the way in, looking a little puzzled.)*
Someone for you, dear.
HENRY For me?
(The man moves down to HENRY, *taking off his hat. This is* DETECTIVE-SERGEANT THATCHER.
He is an apparently easy-going, pleasant man of about forty, but beneath the veneer he is determined and occasionally ruthless. He crosses to HENRY. DORA *moves down R. of the table.)*
THATCHER I'm sorry to trouble you, sir. Are you Mr. Henry Scrubb?

HENRY   Yes, that's right. Who are you?
          (THATCHER *takes out his identification card and shows it.*)
THATCHER Thatcher. Detective-Sergeant Thatcher, C.I.D.
HENRY   Police?
THATCHER (*with a smile*) Er—that's right, sir—yes.
DORA   Here—what do you want with us?
THATCHER I'm coming to that, Mrs. Scrubb. Do you mind if I ask you a few questions, sir?
          (HENRY *rises and puts his newspaper on the mantelpiece.*)
HENRY   What's this all about? I've done nothing wrong.
THATCHER I didn't say you had. Do you know a man named James Franklyn?
          (*A pause.* HENRY *turns to look at* THATCHER.)
HENRY   Franklyn?
THATCHER That's right.
HENRY   No. No, I don't.
THATCHER You're quite sure?
HENRY   'Course I'm sure! I never heard the name.
THATCHER So, if I was to suggest that you went to see Mr. Franklyn at his house last night, you'd say that wasn't true?
HENRY   'Course it's not true! I've never heard of him!
DORA   But Henry——
          (*She stops.* THATCHER *turns to her.*)
THATCHER Yes, Mrs. Scrubb?
DORA   No. It—it doesn't matter.
THATCHER (*turning back to* HENRY) So you can't help us, then?
HENRY   No. I'm afraid not. What—what's it all about, anyway?
THATCHER Last night Mr. Franklyn was murdered.

CURTAIN

ACT II

The action is continuous. HENRY, DORA *and* THATCHER *are in the positions they occupied at the end of Act One.* THATCHER *looks from* HENRY *to* DORA *and back again in silence.*

THATCHER Do you still say you can't help us?
HENRY I don't know anything about it. Why should I?
THATCHER You've never heard of a man named Franklyn?
HENRY I told you! Look, I don't know what we're talking about.
THATCHER We're talking about murder.
HENRY Well, it's nothing to do with me. (*He moves away from* THATCHER *towards* DORA.) Now you just leave us alone, see? I haven't done nothing.
THATCHER (*with a smile*) Well, if you've done nothing then you've nothing to worry about, have you?
DORA (*softly*) Murdered—
THATCHER That's right. He was found dead in his home last night.
DORA It's dreadful. Dreadful—
THATCHER Yes. I think his wife would agree with you.
(HENRY *looks at him.*)
You see, she had to telephone us. And wait there with him until we arrived.
(*There is a pause.*)
HENRY Why did you come here? Why did you think I could help you?
(THATCHER *moves to below the sofa.*)
THATCHER Are you employed at the moment, Mr. Scrubb?
HENRY No, I'm not. What's it to you?
THATCHER Looking for work, then?
HENRY What do *you* think?
THATCHER Been going through the 'Wanted' columns a bit, lately?
HENRY Why not?
(THATCHER *takes a letter out of his pocket.*)
THATCHER Did you write this, sir?
(HENRY *moves to him, takes the letter and looks at it.*)
HENRY How did you get this?

ACT II MURDER FOR THE ASKING

THATCHER Did you write it?
HENRY Yes. I wrote it.
THATCHER And yet you still say you've never heard of a man named Franklyn?
HENRY What are you getting at?
THATCHER That letter was found on Franklyn's body.
(HENRY *turns with the letter to* DORA.)
DORA Isn't that the letter you wrote about that job—the box number?
THATCHER That's correct, Mrs. Scrubb. In reply to an advertisement in the paper. Well, sir?
(HENRY *gives the letter back to* THATCHER.)
HENRY What of it? I was looking for work. There was this ad., see? 'No qualifications,' it said. So I wrote. Nothing wrong in that, is there?
THATCHER And yet you still maintain that you never met this Mr. Franklyn? Are you sure you didn't visit him at his home last night? Perhaps you went to see him about this job?
HENRY No! No! I didn't!
THATCHER You've no idea where he lives?
HENRY No!
(*A pause.* THATCHER *moves thoughtfully towards the fire.*)
THATCHER Where were you last night, sir?
HENRY I—I was here. At home.
THATCHER (*turning*) And you, Mrs. Scrubb? Were you at home?
DORA No. I went to the pictures.
THATCHER I see. (*To* HENRY.) So you were alone here last night during the time your wife was at the pictures, sir?
HENRY Yes.
THATCHER And you stayed in all the evening?
HENRY Yes.
THATCHER Ah! But then, we've only your word for that, haven't we?
HENRY Eh?
THATCHER Only your word that you stayed in all evening.
DORA But, Henry——
THATCHER Yes, Mrs. Scrubb?
DORA (*helpfully*) You did go out, don't you remember, love? You were out when I brought the fish and chips back.
HENRY Oh. Oh, yes. I'd forgotten. (*Crossing behind the sofa to* L. *of it.*) Yes, I did pop out for a—a breath of air. Well, I'd been in all night, see—so I popped out for a breath of air.

(THATCHER *looks at him, then crosses to* L. *of the table.*)
THATCHER (*to* DORA) What time did you get back from the pictures?
DORA I suppose it was about half past ten.
THATCHER So your husband was out at half past ten?
DORA Yes.
THATCHER (*turning back to* HENRY) What time did you get back, sir?
HENRY I don't remember.
THATCHER You don't remember. Oh, come along, sir. Roughly what time?
HENRY I went for a walk. I can't have been very long.
THATCHER (*to* DORA) Perhaps *you* can help us? How long was it after you returned from the pictures before your husband came home?
(DORA *hesitates, looks across at* HENRY.)
DORA I—I'm not sure.
THATCHER Not sure, Mrs. Scrubb? Fish and chips going cold and you're not sure?
DORA I don't remember.
THATCHER (*glancing at* HENRY) Catching, isn't it? Well—had you finished your chips, or what?
DORA Yes. Yes, I'd finished.
THATCHER Finished your chips. Well, that's something anyway. Left your husband's in the oven?
DORA Yes.
THATCHER Bit dried up when you got home, eh, sir?
HENRY I suppose it was about eleven o'clock.
THATCHER Why?
HENRY H'm?
THATCHER Why do you 'suppose' it was about eleven o'clock?
HENRY It must have been about that.
THATCHER But you're not sure?
HENRY No.
THATCHER Didn't see anyone? Anyone you knew. Someone who might remember the time?
HENRY No.
THATCHER Didn't even pop into the local for half a pint and say hello to the landlord?
HENRY No.
THATCHER Pity.
HENRY Why?
THATCHER Would have helped if you had. You know—someone who

could say they saw you at a certain place at a certain time. Policemen like that sort of thing.
(HENRY *turns away* D.L.)
HENRY Why do I have to answer all these questions?
(THATCHER *looks at him for a moment, moves closer to him and speaks quietly.*)
THATCHER You don't *have* to answer them, sir. But a man was killed last night. Now, that may not matter much to you. But it matters to me. Because I'm paid to find out who killed him. I'm paid, see? Paid to get results. And unless I ask questions, I'm not going to get results, am I? The questions may seem unimportant to you, and the answers may not always help me. But if I keep on asking—suddenly it'll all fall into place. (*Pause.*) All right, then, sir, if I ask a few more?
HENRY (*with a sigh*) I suppose so.
THATCHER Thanks.
(HENRY *moves below him to sit on the sofa.*)
Did you ever get a reply, Mr. Scrubb?
HENRY Reply?
THATCHER To that letter you sent to Mr. Franklyn.
HENRY I didn't know it was to Mr. Franklyn when I sent it. It was a box number.
THATCHER (*patiently*) No. I know that. But just the same—did you get a reply?
HENRY No.
THATCHER He never wrote to you at all?
HENRY No.
THATCHER He never communicated with you in any way?
(HENRY *hesitates.* THATCHER *turns to look at him.*)
HENRY No.
THATCHER Aren't you sure about that?
HENRY 'Course I'm sure.
(THATCHER *takes the letter out of his pocket and looks at it casually. He crosses slowly to* D.R.C.)
THATCHER I notice that you put the telephone number here on your letter. He didn't happen to telephone you, by any chance?
HENRY No.
THATCHER H'm. Funny, that. Because Mrs. Franklyn tells me that she overheard a telephone conversation her husband had on Friday afternoon, and apparently he kept on referring to the man at the other end as 'Mr. Scrubb'. So there he was

C

with a letter from a 'Mr. Scrubb' in his pocket, and speaking to a 'Mr. Scrubb' on the telephone. But you'd say that was just coincidence?

HENRY All right! What does it matter if he *did* speak to me? (*A pause.*)

THATCHER (*putting away the letter*) So he *did* telephone you?

HENRY Yes.

(DORA *goes to above the* L. *end of the sofa.*)

DORA Henry, you never told me.

HENRY I didn't think it was important. (*He holds her look as she sits in the chair* D.L.)

THATCHER Now we're getting somewhere. Like I said, you go on asking questions and suddenly the answers begin to fall into place. Eh, Mr. Scrubb?

(HENRY *looks at him.*)

He telephoned you?

HENRY Yes.

THATCHER About the job?

HENRY Yes.

THATCHER And asked you to visit him?

HENRY No.

THATCHER For an interview?

HENRY No!

THATCHER You're quite sure of that? As sure as you were at first about the telephone call?

HENRY He didn't ask me to visit him!

(THATCHER *goes above the sofa.*)

THATCHER But he had to see you about the job, surely? No employer would take you on without an interview. Not just on the strength of a letter. He'd want to see you first. That's commonsense. He'd want to see you. Talk to you.

HENRY He didn't ask me to visit him.

THATCHER Perhaps *he* visited *you*.

(*A pause.* THATCHER *looks between* HENRY *and* DORA. *He moves closer to* HENRY.)

That was it, wasn't it? He visited you.

(HENRY *looks fearfully across at* DORA, *then nods slowly.*)

HENRY (*softly*) Yes.

THATCHER Last night? Would that be it? Last night when your wife was at the pictures? Because *you* didn't meet him, did you, Mrs. Scrubb? You didn't meet Mr. Franklyn?

ACT II   MURDER FOR THE ASKING   35

DORA *(her eyes on* HENRY*)* No.
THATCHER No. I thought not. Shall we settle for last night, then, sir?
HENRY Yes. He came here last night.
THATCHER Right! Now—about what time?
HENRY Soon after Dora had gone to the pictures. About half past seven.
THATCHER He came here to interview you about the job at seven-thirty?
HENRY Yes.
THATCHER What time did he leave?
HENRY I didn't notice.
THATCHER It's funny how definite you are about some things and how indefinite about others. Funny, that, isn't it? Well, did you have a long talk or was the interview over quickly?
HENRY We—we talked quite a bit.
THATCHER Longer than half an hour?
HENRY *(irritated)* No, not longer. About half an hour.
THATCHER So Mr. Franklyn left here about eight o'clock?
HENRY I suppose so, yes.
THATCHER What sort of job was it?
HENRY Er—sort of a—a gardening job.
      (THATCHER *smiles, looks at* DORA *and back to* HENRY.)
THATCHER Are you a gardener, Mr. Scrubb?
HENRY Not an expert, but——
THATCHER Did Mr. Franklyn offer you the job?
HENRY No. He—he didn't think I was suitable.
THATCHER Yet he was still here for half an hour?
HENRY I told you, I'm not sure about how long he was here. It might have been half an hour. It might have been less.
THATCHER So—he advertises a job in a newspaper, says 'no qualifications necessary,' comes out of his way to interview you in your own home and when you say you're no expert he says you're not suitable?
HENRY Yes.
THATCHER It's an unlikely sort of story, isn't it?
HENRY It's what happened!
THATCHER I mean, why should anyone be so secretive about a gardening job? If he'd said what the job was in his advertisement it would have saved you both a lot of trouble, wouldn't it? 'Expert gardener needed'—that's all he had to put. And then you'd have saved yourself a fourpenny stamp.

HENRY I don't know why he didn't put that in! But he didn't! He didn't say what the job was.
THATCHER I wonder why he bothered to put an advertisement in at all? He only had to telephone the Labour Exchange and they'd have sent him a selection of gardeners.
HENRY You don't believe there *was* an advert., do you? Well, I'll show you! It's still here somewhere. (*He rummages in a pile of newspapers that were under one of the sofa cushions.*) I put it here with the others after I'd written the letter. (*He is obviously unable to find it.*)
(THATCHER *waits patiently.*)
Dora, did you move it? It was here. (*He looks up at* THATCHER.) It *was* here.
THATCHER Yes. I'm sure it was. (*He smiles as* HENRY *starts to look again amongst the papers.*) Don't worry. We've already been on to the newspaper. There *was* an advertisement all right.
(HENRY *gazes at him, bewildered and speechless. Then he throws the newspapers down angrily on to the sofa.* THATCHER *rises.*)
Well, thank you very much, sir.
HENRY You've finished, then?
THATCHER Not finished, Mr. Scrubb. Only just beginning.
HENRY Finished with me, I mean.
THATCHER For the moment, sir. For the moment. But I'll be back. (*With a smile.*) You'll find I do tend to come back rather a lot. (*He makes for the door, pauses there for a moment and then returns to* L. *of the sofa.*) Pity about the fish.
HENRY Fish?
THATCHER Last night. I can't bear waste—you know what I mean? Fish and chips drying up like that. (*Turning to* HENRY.) You don't remember the exact time you got home, I suppose?
HENRY I told you!
THATCHER And there you were, Mrs. Scrubb, waiting up with fish and chips.
DORA (*without thinking*) Oh, I went to bed. I wasn't going to— (*She stops.*)
THATCHER Oh? You went to bed?
DORA Yes.
THATCHER Got tired of waiting and went to bed, eh? (*He looks at*

HENRY.) Must have been *very* late, then, Mr. Scrubb. Good morning.
(*He goes out. The front door is heard to slam.*)
HENRY He thinks I did it.
DORA (*rising*) No, he doesn't, Henry——
HENRY He thinks I did it, I tell you!
DORA (*crossing to him*) He can't think that. But he's got to ask questions. Like he said, that's the only way he'll get the truth. (*She sits beside him.*)
HENRY When I tell him the truth he doesn't believe it. He doesn't even *want* to believe it!
DORA That's just silly.
HENRY I've met his type before. All he's thinking of is what's good for *him*, what's going to help *him*. He's going to try and get me for this, you see.
DORA Now listen, Henry, it's no good talking like that——
(*He rises abruptly and moves away.*)
HENRY We're going to get out of here. You pack up your things. We could be out of here and away before he comes back!
DORA (*moving to him*) And do you think he wouldn't find us? He's probably got men outside now. We'd never even get down the road.
HENRY We could try, Dora. We've got to try!
DORA And how do you think it would look—running away like that? Let him ask his questions. He'll find out who really did it. You've just got to be patient.
(*He looks at her for a moment, then subsides into the chair D.R.*)
HENRY Yes. Yes, I suppose so.
DORA We've got no choice.
HENRY No. That's just the trouble.
(*There is quite a long pause.* DORA *takes some of the breakfast things back to the kitchenette.* HENRY *sits still, worried and thoughtful.*)
DORA You never told me you'd had a reply to that letter you sent. I asked you about it last night. You never said you'd had a reply.
HENRY He said he wanted to see me alone. Over the telephone it was. He said—it being business—he'd rather talk about it alone. Man to man—you know.
DORA Business? He was looking for a gardener.

HENRY Yes.
DORA You had to get me out of the way so you could talk about gardening?
HENRY I had to do as he asked, didn't I?
DORA You told me he was selling insurance.
HENRY Well, I—I didn't want you to know that I was no good for the job.
DORA All this secrecy! I don't understand what's been going on. Why did Mr. Franklyn tell Janet that his name was Brandon?
(*Irritated,* HENRY *rises and moves away from her.*)
HENRY I don't know!
DORA And both of you arranging secret meetings——
HENRY It wasn't secret——
DORA Seems a lot of fuss and bother about a little gardening job. (*A pause.*) And what about my latchkey? Was that part of it, too? Did you lift my key so I couldn't come in and find Mr. Franklyn here?
HENRY No, of course not.
DORA Well, you had my key.
HENRY I took it by mistake.
DORA It was in my handbag.
HENRY No, it—it was on the mantelpiece. (*He sits heavily in the armchair.*)
(*There is quite a pause.* DORA *looks out of the window.*)
DORA What sort of a chap was he?
HENRY Who?
DORA This man that was—murdered.
HENRY He was all right. Well-dressed. Quite a smart sort of chap —you know.
DORA You can't really believe it somehow, can you? A man was here last night and now he's dead. You can't believe it. (*She moves into the room a little.*) Why did you pretend you'd never met him? To the police, I mean. Why did you say you'd never heard of him?
HENRY I didn't want to get involved. You know what coppers are like. Once they get on to you they twist everything you say. I didn't want to get involved in it.
DORA Why not? You've done nothing wrong. They only asked if you knew him.
HENRY I wanted to keep out of it. (*He rises to the fireplace.*)

DORA You lied to them, Henry. That's bound to make them suspicious. If you'd come out right away and said he'd been here, he wouldn't have gone on like he did. And the more he went on, the more—— (*She breaks off.*)
HENRY The more what?
DORA Well—the more suspicious it looked. Well, luv, if you had nothing to hide you wouldn't——
(*He turns on her, angrily.*)
HENRY So *you* think I *have* something to hide, is that it?
DORA I'm only saying what it looked like to the police. Look, I'm only trying to help.
HENRY (*moving away from her*) You call this helping? Going on and on all the time! You're as bad as that copper!
DORA We've got to talk about it, Henry——
HENRY Why? Why do we have to talk about it?
DORA Because you aren't telling me the truth, are you? Not all the truth. Not everything.
HENRY There's nothing to tell. This man Franklyn telephoned and asked to see me here last night. He was here for half an hour and then he went. That's all there is. There's nothing more!
(*A short pause.*)
Anything *else* you want to ask me?
DORA Yes. Where did you go last night? You were away a long time. Where did you go?
HENRY I told you—I went for a walk.
DORA And you mean to say you didn't see one person you knew? Not one person who could say what time they saw you?
(*He eludes her and moves to D.C.*)
HENRY No. I didn't see anyone. I went for a walk over the common. I didn't see anyone. What does it matter, anyway? I can go for a walk, can't I? What does it matter?
DORA It matters because you may have to account for the time you were out last night.
(*A pause. He turns to face her.*)
HENRY Account for it?
DORA If you were out during the time Mr. Franklyn was killed, they'll want to know where you were.
HENRY Why? It's nothing to do with me.
DORA Because you were one of the last people to see him alive.

(*A long pause.* HENRY *sinks on to the sofa, does not look at her. She comes to him.*)
You're *not* telling me all the truth, are you? Do you think, after all these years, I don't know when you're hiding something? You didn't tell me everything about last night, did you? (*Pause.*) *Did* you?
(*He turns slowly and looks at her for a moment. Then he shakes his head, unable to find words at first.*)
HENRY (*softly*) No. No, I didn't.
DORA Tell me. What happened? What happened when you spoke to Mr. Franklyn?
(*He looks at her for a moment, then turns away.*)
HENRY It'd be no use.
DORA Why not?
HENRY Sounds—impossible. You'd never believe me. Sounds impossible—
DORA Tell me.
HENRY You won't believe——
DORA What happened last night?
(*Another pause. Then* HENRY *makes a supreme effort.*)
HENRY He—he asked me to—he asked me to murder him. (DORA *is shattered.*)
DORA (*slowly*) He—he asked you to *kill* him?
HENRY Yes. That's why he wanted to see me alone. Why he wanted you out of the way. Why he gave Janet a different name.
DORA (*bewildered*) But—but why should he want you to kill him?
HENRY Well, he was going to die anyhow, see? Heart trouble or something. But he said his wife would get more money from the insurance if he was murdered.
DORA Why didn't you tell the police that?
HENRY How could I? They wouldn't have believed me, would they? (*He looks at her.*) Any more than you do.
DORA (*without conviction*) I believe you, Henry. Of course I do. If you tell me that's what happened, then I believe you.
(*There is a knock at the door of the flat. They react.* HENRY *rises quickly to* D.L.C.)
HENRY (*softly*) It's him! It's that bleeding copper! He's come back.
DORA Now, Henry—how could it be? We heard the front door slam when he left. Don't you remember?

HENRY Oh. Oh, yes. I'd forgotten—
(*She goes and opens the door.* JANET *is there.*)
JANET Here, Dora—you'll never guess!
DORA What?
JANET Haven't you seen it? Look! (*She pushes a newspaper at* DORA.) It's him! The one I told you about! (*Turns to* HENRY.) It's your friend from last night. Spread all over the paper he is. Murdered, it says. (*To* DORA.) And such a lovely suit he had on, too.
DORA Yes. We—we heard about it. (*She moves down L. of the table.*)
JANET Bit of a liar, wasn't he?
DORA A liar?
JANET Well, he said he was in insurance. (*To* HENRY.) He did say that, didn't he? Said he was in insurance and his name was Brandon. Turns out he's retired, quite wealthy and his name's Franklyn. I mean, it doesn't inspire confidence, does it? Such a nice face he had, too. (*Looking at the newspaper.*) Still, now I come to look at his picture he does look a bit shifty. (*Returning to* HENRY.) Here! I suppose they'll want to see you.
HENRY Who?
JANET The police! I mean, they always want to speak to the last people who saw a body alive, don't they? And you must have been *one* of the last, mustn't you? Here! You're about the nearest thing I've ever got to a murderer! (*Apologetically.*) Oh, you know what I mean.
DORA You spoke to him, too, Janet.
JANET Me?
DORA Last night.
JANET Yes, I know. I can't get over it.
DORA So the police will want to speak to you, as well, I expect.
JANET Oh, yes! They already have. It was ever so exciting!
DORA But you've only just——
JANET Outside. Stopped me as I came in. They're out there now.
HENRY Still outside?
JANET Yes.
HENRY What they hanging about out there for?
JANET (*with a giggle*) Keeping an eye on you, of course! Hey! I hope no one was watching when they spoke to me. I mean, it doesn't look nice, does it, being stopped by the

police and cross-examined outside your own front door.
HENRY What did they ask you about?
JANET Whole string of questions! I couldn't see the point of half of them.
HENRY You said you'd seen Mr. Franklyn last night?
JANET Oh, yes. Well, I did, didn't I? So I had to. Do you reckon I'll have to give evidence at the trial?
DORA It depends if your evidence helps them to find the murderer.
JANET Oh, yes. I suppose so. Hope they give me plenty of warning if they do want me. I mean, I'll have to buy a new dress. Do you suppose they've got any idea about who did it?
DORA It's a bit early yet.
JANET Expect they've got their suspicions, though. And you know what the police are like! I reckon once they suspect you you've had it. There was a play about that on the telly the other night. There was this chap, see—all innocent he was—only they wouldn't believe him. And they kept on and on, and the more they asked the more guilty he looked. It was awful! In the end they got him for it. And we all knew he hadn't done it 'cos we'd seen the chap who had—it was that dark one with the funny shaped nose who usually plays doctors. Ever so good, he was.
(*The front door-bell rings.*)
Ooh! I bet that's them again. (*Making for the door.*) I'll go! (*To* HENRY.) You'd better hide, darling. I bet they've come for you! (*She giggles and goes out to the front door.*)
(DORA *moves to* HENRY *urgently.*)
DORA You've got to tell them the truth. You've got to tell the sergeant about last night.
HENRY I can't tell him!
DORA Why not? They can't hurt you as long as you tell the truth.
HENRY If they think I had a reason for killing Franklyn they'll do everything they can to prove I'm guilty.
DORA But you're not guilty——
HENRY Yes, you and I know that—but think what it'd look like to them. Three thousand pounds is a lot of money!
DORA Three thousand pounds?
HENRY Yes. That's what he was going to pay me.
DORA Three thousand pounds?
HENRY It's a lot of money, Dora.

	(They are looking steadily at each other as JANET *comes in, followed by* THATCHER. *She remains there, beaming.* THATCHER *looks back at her, pointedly.)*
THATCHER	Thank you, Miss Gregory.
JANET	A pleasure, I'm sure. I'll be upstairs if you want me. *(She goes out, closing the door.)*
DORA	You weren't away long.
THATCHER	I said I'd be back, didn't I? *(He puts his hat on the table.)*
HENRY	Didn't expect you as soon as this, though.
THATCHER	*(smiling)* That's the secret of my success. People think I've gone for good, and then suddenly there I am—back again. I won't keep you above five minutes. That will be all right, sir?
HENRY	Looks as if it'll have to be, don't it? *(*DORA *sits in the armchair.)*
THATCHER	I've just been in touch with Headquarters, and the pathologist has now been able to tell us pretty accurately what time Franklyn died.
HENRY	Oh?
THATCHER	Somewhere between nine-thirty and ten-thirty last night. While you were having your breath of air.
HENRY	What about it?
THATCHER	It's a matter of eliminating some of the possibilities. If you can prove that you were somewhere else between nine-thirty and ten-thirty last night, then we shan't have to trouble you any more.
HENRY	And if I can't?
THATCHER	*(with a sigh)* We'll just have to go on asking questions.
HENRY	I've told you before. I went for a walk on the common.
THATCHER	What time did you leave here?
HENRY	I dunno.
THATCHER	Nine o'clock? Would it be about nine o'clock?
HENRY	It might have been.
THATCHER	It *was*, wasn't it, sir? You see, somebody heard you go out. She—er—they are quite sure it was nine o'clock.
HENRY	What if it was?
THATCHER	And you admit you got back here about eleven o'clock?
HENRY	Yes.
THATCHER	How long would you say it would take to get from here to Franklyn's house? *(*HENRY *looks at* DORA, *crosses to* THATCHER.*)*

HENRY What are you trying to say?
THATCHER How long it would take to get from here to Franklyn's house.
HENRY I didn't go to his house.
THATCHER (*patiently*) But—for the sake of argument—how long would it take you?
(*A pause,* HENRY *sees the trap.*)
HENRY I can't tell you.
THATCHER Why not?
HENRY I don't know where Mr. Franklyn lives.
(THATCHER *smiles.*)
THATCHER But you wrote to him.
HENRY It was a Box Number. Don't you remember?
THATCHER Of course! That was silly of me, wasn't it? Well, *I'll* tell *you*. I reckon it would take forty minutes, door to door.
HENRY Well?
THATCHER Well, suppose—again for the sake of argument—that you *did* go to Franklyn's house last night. If you left here at nine o'clock, you'd be there by nine-forty. You could stay at his house until as late as ten-twenty and still be back here by eleven o'clock.
HENRY Yes, I could.
THATCHER That way you would have been at his house between the times the pathologist has given us.
HENRY Yes.
THATCHER (*with a smile*) Fits well, doesn't it?
HENRY Yes, it all fits. Except for one thing.
THATCHER What's that?
HENRY I didn't go to Mr. Franklyn's house and I didn't kill him.
THATCHER That's precisely why I want you to tell me exactly where you did go last night—so that we can eliminate the possibility.
HENRY I've told you—I went for a walk!
THATCHER (*moving close to* HENRY) Yes, but *where*, Mr. Scrubb? *Where* did you walk? You say you walked on the common. On the way you spoke to nobody. You saw nobody. Between nine-thirty and eleven at night there was nobody about. Not one single person who might recollect having seen you.
HENRY (*vehemently*) Do you think I don't *wish* I'd met somebody?

ACT II   MURDER FOR THE ASKING   45

                Do you think I don't *want* to find someone who saw me? But there was no one. Just no one.
THATCHER Maybe not even you, Mr. Scrubb? Perhaps even you were somewhere else?
                (*They look at each other for a moment.* HENRY, *breathing heavily, sinks on to the sofa.* THATCHER *breaks away and wanders upstage a little.*)
                (*Casually.*) Did you telephone anyone last night?
HENRY Telephone?
THATCHER From the call-box in the hall out there.
HENRY No. No, I didn't.
THATCHER Shortly after Mr. Franklyn left?
HENRY No.
THATCHER You didn't telephone a friend, or something?
HENRY No.
THATCHER You didn't make a 'phone call at all?
HENRY No!
THATCHER You're sure of that?
HENRY You think I don't know if I made a 'phone call?
THATCHER (*moving above the sofa to L. of it*) Supposing somebody said they saw you?
HENRY I never made no 'phone call. I tell you!
DORA Leave him alone, can't you? Leave him alone!
THATCHER I'm sorry, Mrs. Scrubb. I'm only trying to get at the truth. And I can't when it's clouded all the time by little—lapses of memory. (*He turns to* HENRY.) You made a 'phone call from out there last night. We know you did because Miss Gregory in the upstairs flat said she came down the stairs about a quarter to nine to use the 'phone—only you were already using it.
HENRY She must have been mistaken.
THATCHER No. She was quite sure it was you.
HENRY I didn't make a 'phone call last night!
                (THATCHER *smiles, moves closer to* HENRY *and speaks casually and quietly.*)
THATCHER It wouldn't have mattered very much if you had, would it, sir? Might have been to a friend of yours—anything. Not very important whether you did or you didn't.
                (HENRY *looks up at him.*)
HENRY (*bitterly*) No. No, I suppose not.
THATCHER I do wish you'd tell the truth. About everything, the im-

portant things *and* the unimportant. Let's go back, shall we, to the conversation you had with Mr. Franklyn—?
(DORA *moves quickly to* HENRY.)

DORA   Henry—you've got to tell him! You've got to!

THATCHER   Has he been holding something back, Mrs. Scrubb?

HENRY   I've told you everything——

DORA   For God's sake, Henry, tell him! Tell him before it's too late!

HENRY   I've nothing to tell——!

DORA   (*turning to* THATCHER) Sergeant—Mr. Franklyn didn't want a gardener——

HENRY   Dora, don't! You mustn't!

DORA   (*loudly*) He wanted my husband to kill him!
(*There is a long pause.* DORA, *crying, collapses into the armchair.* HENRY *is absolutely still.* THATCHER *watches them thoughtfully for a moment, then he crosses slowly and sits next to* HENRY. *He takes out a packet of cigarettes.*)

THATCHER   Cigarette, sir?
(HENRY *turns to look at* THATCHER, *casually offering a cigarette.*)

HENRY   No. No, thanks.

THATCHER   Do you mind if I do? (*He lights a cigarette in silence.*)
(DORA'S *crying subsides gradually.*)

HENRY   (*quietly*) Don't believe it, do you?

THATCHER   I'm trained to keep an open mind. Tell me more.

HENRY   (*with resignation*) He—he said he was going to die in six months—some heart trouble. He said something about—about an insurance policy—how his wife would get twice the money if he—if he was murdered. So—he was wanting to pay me three thousand pounds to do it.

THATCHER   Did you agree to the suggestion?

HENRY   Of course I didn't! What the hell do you take me for? I told him he was mad and to get off out of here!

THATCHER   I see. And that was the last you saw of him?

HENRY   Yes!
(THATCHER *holds his look for a moment, then faces front thoughtfully.*)
I didn't kill him. You've got to believe me! I didn't kill him.
(THATCHER *looks at* HENRY *steadily for a moment, then he rises and collects his hat from the table.*)

THATCHER You won't be going away, or anything, will you?
HENRY You *don't* believe me, do you?
THATCHER I only believe evidence, sir. And you must admit, it does sound a little unlikely.
HENRY I know it does, but it's true! It's what happened!
THATCHER Well, at the moment I only have your word, and that hasn't been too reliable up to now, has it, sir? I'll check with his insurance company, and then we shall know, shan't we? Even if it is true, I don't expect *Mrs.* Franklyn is overjoyed. I expect she'd sooner have had her husband. Even if it was only for six months. (*He starts for the door.*)
HENRY It's true, I tell you!
THATCHER Maybe it is. Maybe it is. *If* it is, then—then it gives you a motive, doesn't it? (*He moves to the door.*) It's all right, I know the way.
(*He goes out and after a moment we hear the front door slam.*)
HENRY Well, I hope you're satisfied. Now see where you've landed me! The truth didn't help much, did it?
(DORA *rises and crosses above* HENRY *to R. of the sofa.*)
DORA It will, luv. You must believe that. He'll find out that what you said was true and then everything'll be all right.
HENRY You don't know what you've done. You just don't know.
DORA He's bound to be a bit suspicious at first. I mean, you must admit, it does sound a little unlikely, doesn't it?
HENRY But it's what happened! Right here in this room. It's what he asked me to do. Dora, surely *you* believe me?
(DORA *turns away from him, avoiding his eyes.*)
DORA I only said it sounded unlikely, that's all. Like I said, he'll check your story and when he finds out that it's true, then —(*Faltering.*) everything will be all right.
HENRY Will it? A motive, that's what he said, didn't he? Up till I told him the truth he was puzzled. He knew I had the opportunity, but he couldn't think *why* I should do it. Well, now he knows. Three thousand pounds. That's a good enough reason. Isn't it, Dora?
(DORA *turns and looks at him for a moment.*)
DORA Yes. Yes, Henry. That's a good enough reason.
(*A pause. Then she breaks the atmosphere.*)

I'll have to think about lunch. It's getting late. (*She goes to the kitchenette and begins sorting out a few things.*) I'll have to go out to the shops this afternoon. I've nothing in for to-morrow.

(HENRY *is sitting dejectedly, gazing ahead.*)

HENRY Dora——

DORA Yes, luv?

HENRY Supposing—supposing they *never* believe me? You know —never believe I'm innocent—what'll happen?

DORA I don't know.

HENRY Will they arrest me?

DORA (*trying to pass it off lightly*) They're not going to arrest you simply because you tell a couple of lies.

HENRY They might think I was hiding something.

DORA (*moving to him*) They'd have to have proof, Henry. They'd have to prove that you were there at the time of the murder and all that. And you weren't there—we both know that—so you've nothing to worry about. It'll be all right, you see. They'll find out what really happened.

HENRY (*unconvinced*) Yes. Yes, I expect so.

(DORA *goes back to the kitchenette and busies herself. There is quite a pause.*)

DORA Are you quite sure about the 'phone, luv?

HENRY Eh?

DORA About not using the 'phone last night.

HENRY (*rising*) Look—I didn't use the bloody 'phone. I told you. Want me to get out the Bible—swear on that? (*He moves away L.*)

DORA There's no need to be like that, Henry. I only wondered. I mean, it's not likely that Janet would say she'd seen you if she hadn't.

HENRY She was mistaken, that's all. You going to take her word against mine?

DORA I just thought you might have forgotten.

HENRY She came down the stairs and saw someone on the telephone and assumed it was me. Maybe it was that new bloke on the third floor. I don't know. But she was mistaken. (*Pause.*) Or else she made it up.

DORA Janet? She'd never do a thing like that.

HENRY Oh, wouldn't she? I've made no bones of the fact that I think she's a bloody nuisance—barging in and out of here,

all hours of the day and night—so I reckon she'd jump at a chance to pay me back.
DORA How on earth could she think she was paying you back by saying she saw you make a 'phone call?
HENRY I don't know!
DORA She never even thought about it. She just said what happened. She just said what she saw.
HENRY (*loudly*) All right! All right! So she saw me making a 'phone call! Does that make me a murderer?
(*There is a long pause.* HENRY *is breathing heavily.* DORA *moves in to him.*)
DORA (*quietly*) Why did you say you hadn't? Why did you tell him another lie?
HENRY I—I was frightened. I didn't want to make him even more suspicious.
DORA But he said himself it wasn't important. There's nothing wrong in making a 'phone call.
HENRY I was frightened he might have asked me who it was I was 'phoning.
DORA What would that matter? It might have been to anyone. (*He avoids her eyes and sits on the sofa.*) Who were you 'phoning, luv?
(HENRY *turns and looks at her steadily.*)
HENRY Are you quite sure you want to go on with this? Are you quite sure?
(*She holds his gaze for a moment.*)
DORA Yes, Henry.
HENRY I was 'phoning Mr. Franklyn.
(*A long pause.* DORA *looks at him for a moment, uncomprehending.*)
DORA But why? Why, Henry? Why should you want to 'phone Mr. Franklyn? He'd only left you about an hour before.
HENRY Yes. I know.
DORA Then—why?
HENRY I—I wanted to see him again.
(DORA *is suddenly fearful, suddenly uncertain of* HENRY.)
DORA Did he answer the 'phone?
HENRY Yes. (*In a flat voice.*) He said I was to go to his house right away.
(*She sits beside him, her eyes searching his face in fear.*)
DORA And—did you? (*A pause, then urgently.*) Henry—did you?

D

(*There is a moment, then he nods, without looking at her.*)
HENRY Yes. I went to his house.

CURTAIN

ACT III
SCENE I

Early the same evening.
When the curtain rises the stage is empty, then DORA *comes in, carrying a bag of groceries. She stops in the open door and calls down the hall.*

DORA Janet!
      (*She comes into the flat, leaving the door open. She puts the groceries down in the kitchenette and starts to take off her coat.*
      JANET *comes in from the hall. She looks about cautiously.*)
JANET Is he back?
DORA No. Still out.
JANET Oh, that's all right, then. (*She closes the door.*) You were a long time.
      (DORA *goes to light the gas fire.*)
DORA Yes. I had a few things to do. Janet, did you leave the front door open when you came in?
JANET Me? No.
DORA Are you sure? It was wide open. Anyone could have walked in.
JANET I expect it was the old devil on the top floor. He's always doing that. Wouldn't make much odds, anyhow. Nobody'd want to pinch anything *I*'ve got—if you know what I mean.
      (DORA *sits wearily in the armchair.*)
      Can I get you something? Cup of coffee, or something?
DORA No, thanks. I'll be all right in a minute. Just a bit tired, that's all.
JANET I'm not surprised. It's been a worry for you, hasn't it? That copper doesn't half go on, popping in and out of here like a Jack-in-the-Box. I mean, he's lovely really, but it does put us all under a bit of a cloud—all those questions. Never mind. I expect it's all over. They must have found out who did it by now.

DORA *(trying to brighten up)* Yes, I expect they have.
(JANET *sits on the arm of the sofa.*)

JANET Quite exciting, really, isn't it? You know what I mean? I was saying to my friend only this afternoon, 'It's like being in the pictures—you never know what's going to happen next'! I mean, last night when I came in here and spoke to that Mr. Franklyn, I never thought he'd be dead the next minute. Well, you don't, do you? Henry gone to football?

DORA Er—no. No, he hasn't.

JANET No. Poor soul. Don't suppose he felt like it. Can't be much fun for him having the police in and out like that. *(With a sigh.)* I wish they'd think of some more questions for me.
(The door opens and HENRY *comes in. He sees* JANET *and is not pleased.*)

JANET *(cheerfully)* Hullo, Lover Boy!

HENRY You here for a change?

JANET Ooh! Pardon me for living, I'm sure! You don't have to worry—I'm just going.

HENRY Good.

JANET Charming! *(To* DORA.*)* Deep down I'm sure he fancies me really. See you later. *(As she passes* HENRY.*)* Goodbye, darling! *(She goes.)*

HENRY I wish she'd keep her nose out of here.
(He moves down into the room, taking off his raincoat. DORA *watches him for a moment.*)

DORA No luck?

HENRY H'm? *(He puts his raincoat on the chair above the table.)*

DORA The man on Franklyn's list.

HENRY Oh. No. I wish to God Franklyn had never made a bloody list. *(He takes the list out of his pocket and moves down below the sofa.)*

DORA Did you find out where he lived?

HENRY Yes. I found that all right. But he wasn't there. I spoke to his wife.

DORA Did she know about Mr. Franklyn?

HENRY Oh, yes. Her husband had written a letter to the box number—just like I did—and Franklyn had telephoned him.
(She crosses to him excitedly.)

DORA So it might have been *him!*

HENRY No. He never met Franklyn. He got a job on a ship. Sailed for Gib yesterday morning—and Franklyn was still alive then.
DORA *(deflated)* Oh. So that's one name off the list.
HENRY Yes. Just leaves the two of us, don't it?
DORA Perhaps we should have given that list of names to the police? Let *them* investigate?
HENRY What? And admit I was in Franklyn's house last night? They'd never believe I only went there to get this list of names. If they can prove I was in that house that's all the evidence they'll need! No. I'll have to find this other bloke —Fred Pender.
DORA I already have.
HENRY What?
DORA I already have.
HENRY You?
DORA Yes.
HENRY *(sharply)* You shouldn't have done that, Dora. You shouldn't have done that.
DORA Well—I—I thought it would help.
HENRY Yes—I know—but it—it might have been dangerous.
DORA Do you think that matters? I want to help, Henry.
HENRY *(more gently)* Yes. I know.
DORA I couldn't find him, anyway. I went to that address—he's living in digs. But they said he wasn't there.
HENRY Lucky for you he wasn't.
DORA I traced him as far as a billiard hall where he'd been working part time. The man there said he'd be in later, so I left a message asking him to call here.
HENRY *(alarmed)* Call here?
DORA Well, what else could I do? I said it was important.
HENRY You shouldn't have given him this address, Dora. You shouldn't have done that.
(*The door-bell goes. They look at each other.*)
DORA Could that be him now?
HENRY Could be. (*He makes for the door.*)
DORA *(following him, urgently)* Be careful, Henry, won't you? I mean—if he is the man who killed Mr. Franklyn, he'll be desperate.
HENRY I'm desperate, too, luv. I've got to find him. I've just *got* to. (*He goes out to the front door.* DORA *goes to R. of the table.*

After a moment THATCHER *walks in. He carries a small attaché case.* HENRY *follows him in.*)

(*Sarcastically.*) Don't know why you don't move in. There's a bed-sit going on the top floor, you know.

THATCHER I might at that, Mr. Scrubb. I might at that. (*He moves* D.L.)
HENRY (*to* DORA) He wants me to go to the station.
DORA Why?
THATCHER Just a routine matter. You see, I'd like to have your fingerprints taken. I presume you'll have no objection?
HENRY Why do you want them?
THATCHER Well, *somebody* was in Franklyn's house last night before he was killed. We've managed to identify most of the prints we found, but there is one set that we can't account for. So it's—well, a matter of eliminating the possibilities again.
HENRY I see.
THATCHER So if we can compare your prints with those found in the house and we find that they *don't* match, then you'll be a bit more in the clear, won't you, sir?
HENRY Yes.
THATCHER I'm only trying to help, sir. Oh, by the way, we checked with Franklyn's insurance company. There was no clause such as you suggest.

(HENRY *moves below the sofa to* THATCHER.)

HENRY What?
DORA Henry——!
HENRY But there *must* be!
THATCHER We've checked very thoroughly.
HENRY But he told me——
THATCHER It comes back to the old thing, though, doesn't it? We've only your word for what Mr. Franklyn told you.
HENRY But—it's true.
THATCHER Is it? (THATCHER *makes for the door.*) Well, shall we go and see about those fingerprints?

(HENRY *moves away, thoughtfully.* THATCHER *waits, watching him.*)
Well, sir?

HENRY You can save yourself the trouble.
THATCHER Oh?
HENRY (*turning to face him*) I *did* go to Mr. Franklyn's house last night.

SCENE I   MURDER FOR THE ASKING

(THATCHER *moves back from the doorway, puts his hat and case on the table.*)

THATCHER Well, well!
HENRY But I didn't murder him.
THATCHER What *did* you do?
HENRY I went to get something.
(*He gets out of his pocket the list of names which* FRANKLYN *showed to him in Act I. He takes it to* THATCHER. *They meet below the sofa.*)
There! I went to get that.
THATCHER (*studying the paper*) What have we here?
HENRY Last night, Mr. Franklyn showed me that list of names. He said those were the three people he was seeing about this job he had to offer.
THATCHER Now, look here, I told you——
HENRY It's true, I tell you!
THATCHER Why should you want to get this list back from him?
HENRY I thought it might—incriminate me.
THATCHER In what?
HENRY In murder.
THATCHER How did you know there was going to *be* a murder?
HENRY (*getting flustered*) I—I didn't! But I thought—suppose one of the other people on that list—suppose they agree to what he asked—suppose he *is* murdered. Then my name on a piece of paper in his pocket would involve me right away.
THATCHER So you'd forgotten about the letter you wrote to him? The one we found on the body. The one that brought me here in the first place.
HENRY Yes. I'd forgotten about that.
THATCHER If you were so innocent, why should you care about a few questions?
HENRY I *am* innocent! (*Then quietly.*) But *you're* not going to believe me, are you?
THATCHER It's not a question of what I believe, Mr Scrubb. It's a question of proof..
(*There is quite a pause.* THATCHER *is looking at the piece of paper.* HENRY, *breathing heavily, moves away to the fireplace.*)
(*Without looking up.*) How did you get this, anyway? Pick his pocket when you got there?

HENRY Well—yes.
THATCHER You knew the opportunity would present itself?
HENRY I had to take a gamble on that.
THATCHER And the gamble paid off?
HENRY Yes.
THATCHER How very lucky for you. What did you say to him when you got to his house?
HENRY I said I was thinking it over.
THATCHER His offer?
HENRY Yes.
THATCHER You told him you were prepared to murder him?
HENRY Yes. But I only said that so he'd let me in!
THATCHER I see. Go on.
HENRY He talked quite a bit. He even offered me more money and all that. Then he went out of the room to fetch something. His jacket was on the back of a chair——
THATCHER And you seized your opportunity?
HENRY Yes.
THATCHER How long were you there?
HENRY Only about ten minutes.
THATCHER And then you came home?
HENRY Yes. I had to wait a long time for a 'bus.
THATCHER I see. (*He moves in silence to the small attaché case and brings it down to* HENRY.) Is this yours, sir?
HENRY No.
THATCHER Have you never seen it before?
(*A pause.* HENRY *does not reply.*)
It was found in Mr. Franklyn's house after he'd been murdered. The contents are rather interesting.
(*He opens the case. It contains a number of silver articles—candlesticks, ashtrays, etc.*)
Quite a nice little collection. You did say you'd never seen this case before?
(*There is a pause.* HENRY *sinks into the chair* D.L. *and continues haltingly.*)
HENRY I saw it last night at Mr. Franklyn's house. That was what he went out of the room to get. Then he put those things inside—said I could have those as well as the money if I did as he asked.
THATCHER (*with a smile*) Very generous of him. We also found fingerprints on this case. (*He closes the attaché case.*) Shall I tell

SCENE I   MURDER FOR THE ASKING   57

you what *I* think happened last night? Franklyn came here to see you about a job. Oh, he *was* looking for a gardener, by the way. His wife has confirmed that. But he told you that you were unsuitable. You were angry, and you were poor, and you followed him back to his house.

HENRY No! That's not true!
THATCHER You plead with him to give you another chance because you need the work. He lets you in and talks to you, tries to make you see reason. And then you see these things— (*Indicating the attaché case.*)—worth a lot of money, eh, Mr. Scrubb? Money you badly need.
HENRY But it isn't what happened——!
THATCHER Isn't it? A quick blow on the back of the head when he's turned away from you and Franklyn is on the floor. You grab a few things and put them into his suitcase, but then you find Franklyn is coming round and he tries to stop you going. There's a struggle, and the next thing you know you've grabbed the paper knife from the desk and Franklyn is dead.
HENRY That's not true! *You* know that's not true!
(*A short pause.* THATCHER *smiles.*)
THATCHER It fits the facts, though, doesn't it? And it sounds a little more likely than your story. Don't you agree?
HENRY It—isn't—what—happened!
THATCHER We shall have to find out, shan't we? Can we go now, then? (*He goes to collect his hat from the table.*)
HENRY Are you arresting me?
THATCHER Oh, no. Simply asking you to come to the station for further questioning.
DORA Haven't you asked him enough questions already?
THATCHER Perhaps he'll answer them better at the station.
HENRY How long will I be gone?
THATCHER That depends on you. Come along. (*He moves up to the door and goes out, leaving the door open.*)
(HENRY *goes to* DORA. *They gaze ineffectually at each other. He takes his raincoat and makes for the door.*)
HENRY I'll not be long, luv.
DORA No. All right, Henry.
(*He goes out, closing the door behind him. The front door is heard to slam.* DORA *is near to tears. She moves across below the sofa, slightly dazed, then on an impulse she goes*

quickly up to the door as if to follow them. She pulls the door open and gasps with horror. A large, rough-looking man stands in the doorway. DORA *backs away slightly. The man closes the door and looks at her.*)

DORA Who are you?
PENDER Pender. Fred Pender.
DORA How did you get in?
PENDER The front door was open. I've been waiting down the passage out there. I didn't like to come in before. Thought I'd hang about till it was all clear. Are you his wife?
(DORA *gazes at him, speechless.*)
Yes. I expect you are.
(*She backs away further.*)
DORA (*softly*) Get out of here—
PENDER Now what sort of a reception is that? I was asked, you know. The message said it was important. Now, why was your husband so keen to find me, eh? Tell me that.
DORA I—I don't know—
PENDER Doesn't take you into his confidence, eh? Is that it? (*He comes closer.*) Someone went to my digs, see—then to the billiard hall. Proper little Sherlock Holmes. They—they said it was a woman. Wouldn't have been you by any chance, would it? All right—let's have it—what's in this for *me*?
DORA (*retreating to the fireplace*) You'd—you'd better go——
PENDER Oh, no, lady. I'm not going. Reckon there's something in this for me, and I want to know what. The message said for me to look him up. Said it was important. Now, what I want to know is—did it mean important to *him*, or important to *me*? There's a difference, you see. Anyhow, thought I'd take a chance on it.
DORA Please go.
PENDER Not frightened, are you? Frightened of me? Why should you be frightened of me? Eh?
DORA Why didn't you come in just now when my husband was here?
(PENDER *sits on the* L. *arm of the sofa.*)
PENDER Well, I was going to, see—once that bird from upstairs left, but then this other bloke turned up and—well, I didn't want to interrupt, see? Mind if I smoke?
DORA Er—no. No, I don't mind.

SCENE I   MURDER FOR THE ASKING   59

PENDER That's better! You're getting more friendly now. (*He takes out a battered old cigarette, but cannot find any matches. He looks at her.*) Matches?
DORA Over there.
PENDER (*looking about*) Oh, yes. Ta. (*He goes to get matches from the sideboard, lights his cigarette and puts the box in his pocket.*) What's it all about, then?
DORA I told you, I don't know. Look, couldn't you come back when my husband's home? He may be a long time.
PENDER I can wait. Now I'm here I may as well wait. You got any more cigarettes? This is my last.
DORA No—no, I haven't.
(*He smiles, enjoying her discomfort.*)
PENDER Then I'll have to do without, won't I?
(*A pause. He smokes, looking at her thoughtfully. She is nervous, apprehensive.*)
Is he in some sort of trouble?
DORA No—no, of course not.
PENDER 'Cos if he wants to borrow money he's come to the wrong bloke, see? (*He chuckles and moves away to the table.*)
DORA No, it isn't that.
(*He turns to look at her.*)
PENDER I thought you said you didn't know what it was.
DORA Well, I—I know he doesn't want to borrow money.
PENDER That's all right, then. You see, I'm a bit short of the ready myself. I was—like—hoping there was going to be something in this for me, see? You know what I mean?
(DORA *moves to above the sofa, her confidence returning.*)
DORA Well—er—there might be.
PENDER Oh?
DORA I'm not sure, of course.
PENDER Not sure but there might be?
DORA Yes.
PENDER That's good enough for me.
(*A pause.* PENDER *prowls across to the fireplace. She watches him anxiously.*)
Wonder how he got hold of my name.
DORA I don't know.
PENDER Always interests me, you see, how people get hold of my name.

(*Gradually* DORA *is gaining courage. She moves down to R. of the sofa.*)

DORA (*suddenly*) Have you ever heard of James Franklyn?
(*He turns and faces her.*)
PENDER What do you know about him?
DORA Do you know him?
PENDER (*after a pause*) No.
DORA But you wrote to him, didn't you?
PENDER What's that to you?
DORA You wrote to him?
PENDER I wrote a letter, yes—but I didn't know what his name was then. It sounded interesting. Plenty of money—you know.
DORA (*moving below the sofa*) Then he telephoned you—asked you to go and see him?
PENDER Look, what is all this?
DORA Was it last night? Did he ask you to go and see him last night?
(*He comes towards her a little.*)
PENDER Yes. Yes, he did. Who the hell are you? You're going on like one of them female coppers. What's it to do with you who I go and see?
DORA Did you?
PENDER Eh?
DORA Did you go and see him?
PENDER Look, lady—I don't know what all this is leading up to, but I don't like people poking their noses in my business. Okay? Maybe you were right. I'd better come back when your husband's here. (*He makes for the door and opens it.*)
DORA (*moving urgently to L. of the sofa*) Did you go and see Mr. Franklyn last night?
(PENDER *stops, turns to look at her for a moment, closes the door and moves down to her. He speaks quietly.*)
PENDER Yes. Yes, I went to see him. *Now* are you satisfied? I went to see him. But nobody answered the door. Okay?
(*He looks at her steadily for a moment, then turns and makes for the door again.*)
DORA (*desperately*) So you don't know if he was still alive at a quarter past ten?
(PENDER *stops and turns.*)
PENDER Still alive?
DORA Mr. Franklyn was murdered last night. Didn't you know?

SCENE I MURDER FOR THE ASKING

(There is quite a pause.)
PENDER No, I didn't know that. What are you trying to do? You trying to involve me in something? Is that what this is all about? You trying to involve me? *(He comes nearer to her.)* Look, I didn't know he was dead until you told me. I never even saw this bloke Franklyn. I never got no answer when I rang the bell. I never went into his house. So whatever happened, it's nothing to do with me!
DORA Would you tell the same thing to the police?
PENDER You *are* in trouble, aren't you? Lady, it's your affair. I ain't done nothing, so I ain't got nothing to worry about.
DORA Let's call the police, then!
PENDER *(moving in close to her)* You're either brave or barmy. Suppose I *was* involved in this—do you think I'd *let* you call the police?
DORA They think my husband killed Mr. Franklyn.
(A pause. PENDER *smiles.)*
PENDER Oh, I see! And you're trying to push it on to someone else, eh? Well, you picked the wrong person. I'm as clean as a whistle.
DORA I *know* he didn't do it!
PENDER You'll get used to the idea in time. All right now if I go? *(He moves to the door.)*
DORA *(in final desperation)* How do I know you're telling the truth?
PENDER *(turning angrily)* Don't push your luck, lady! I've been very patient with you, and now I'm off. If your old man's done a murder, it's got nothing to do with me! Franklyn was alive all right when *I* left there! I didn't do him in! *(He angrily makes for the door again.)*
DORA How do you know?
(He turns at the door.)
PENDER Eh?
DORA How do you know he was alive if you didn't see him?
(He stands absolutely motionless for a few seconds, then moves slowly towards her. Suddenly the courage of desperation has left her, and she is only a frightened woman again. She retreats round L. of the sofa to below it.)
I—I'm going to tell the Police.
PENDER *(following as she retreats)* I wouldn't do that, lady. I wouldn't do that if I was you.

DORA   I'm going to tell the police.
PENDER Oh, no you're not.
       (*She suddenly starts to move quickly for the door, but he grabs her. She screams, a loud, frightened scream, as the lights* FADE *quickly to* BLACKOUT.)

CURTAIN

ACT III
SCENE II

An hour later.
DORA *is on the sofa with her feet up, sipping a cup of tea.* JANET *is at the table pouring a cup for herself.*

JANET   You didn't half give me a fright! I thought you were being murdered. How do you feel, love?
DORA   (*a little dazed*) I'm—I'm all right now.
JANET   Haven't got any brandy, I'm afraid. Still, a cup of tea's just as good, isn't it?
DORA   Thank you. I feel better all ready.
        (JANET *brings her tea to L. of the sofa.*)
JANET   I was sitting upstairs when all of a sudden I heard it. You didn't half scream, you know. So down I came, fast as lightning. Who was he? A burglar?
DORA   I—I don't know. I expect so.
JANET   Well, he shot out of here fast enough. Almost knocked me over as I came in. (*She sits on the arm of the sofa.*)
DORA   You've been a great help, Janet.
JANET   That's all right, love. I don't mind telling you, when I came through that door and saw you lying there on the floor, I said to myself, 'Look at her,' I said, 'she's snuffed it,' I said. And you should have seen me getting you on to the sofa—talk about laugh! I mean, you don't look what I call a heavy woman. You know what I mean? Heavy bones, I suppose that's what it is. Heavy bones. Here, let me get you some more tea.

SCENE II MURDER FOR THE ASKING   63

DORA   No. I won't have any more, thanks.
JANET It's no trouble.
DORA   I feel all right, now. Really.
JANET Okay. I'll just put these things across here out of your way.
       (*She takes the cups and saucers and tea-pot, etc. to the kitchenette.* DORA *sits up slowly.*)
       You sure you're all right?
DORA   Yes. Yes, thanks.
JANET Hadn't you better call the police?
DORA   The police?
JANET To report the burglary.
DORA   Oh, yes. Yes, I—I suppose so.
JANET Shall I do it for you? I should have done it before, but I didn't like to leave you, the state you were in.
DORA   No, it's all right. I'll do it, Janet. Not that it makes any difference, now.
JANET Still, it's got to be done. I mean, you never know. They might be able to catch him.
DORA   Yes. Yes, they might.
       (*The front door-bell goes.*)
JANET That's your bell, isn't it?
DORA   Yes. (*She looks a little apprehensive.*)
JANET You stay here. I'll see who it is.
DORA   (*as* JANET *reaches the door*) He—he wouldn't come back, would he?
JANET Come back? The rate he was going he'll be halfway to Scotland, by now!
       (*She goes out to the front door.* DORA *rises, feels a little unsteady, blinks to clear her head and crosses slowly to the fireplace.* JANET *returns.*)
JANET (*confidentially*) It's someone for you.
DORA   For me?
JANET Says it's important.
       (*A well-dressed woman in her early 40's comes in.*)
DORA   Oh. Thank you, Janet.
JANET (*going*) I'll be upstairs, if you want me. Just give a shout.
       (*She gives the visitor a warning glance and goes off.*
       The visitor glances around the room, then moves slowly down towards DORA, *who eyes her apprehensively.*)
DORA   If you're one of them Jehovah's Witnesses, I don't want to **know!**

RITA *(with a little smile)* No, it's nothing like that. Look—er—I do hope you don't mind my coming to see you.
(RITA *is a gently spoken woman with a friendly personality.*)
DORA It depends what you want.
RITA You *are* Mrs. Scrubb, aren't you?
DORA Yes. That's right. And who are you, may I ask?
RITA I'm—Rita Franklyn.
DORA Franklyn? You—you mean—you're——?
RITA Yes. That's right. I'm his wife.
(*There is quite a pause as they look at each other.*)
DORA What you come here for? What you want with me?
RITA To talk. I—I just wanted to talk. That's all.
DORA What have *we* got to talk about?
RITA Please. Just for a moment.
DORA *(embarrassed)* Well—well, I suppose it's all right. You'd better sit down.
RITA Thank you. *(She sits on the sofa.)*
DORA It's not very tidy, I'm afraid.
RITA That's all right.
(DORA *hovers, tentatively.*)
DORA *(after a pause)* Would you like some tea?
RITA No, no—please don't trouble!
DORA There's some made.
RITA Well, in that case, thank you.
(DORA *goes and gets a cup and saucer and pours some tea.*)
DORA Sugar?
RITA No, thanks.
(DORA *brings the cup of tea to* RITA.)
Thank you. *(A pause. She sips the tea.)* H'm. Very nice.
DORA It's funny, you know. You're not a bit what I expected.
RITA Aren't I? What did you think I'd be like?
DORA Oh, I dunno—sort of harder, I suppose. I dunno why. But you're—you're gentle, aren't you?
(RITA *smiles and sips her tea. A pause.*)
Look—look, I'm ever so sorry.
RITA Sorry?
DORA You know.
RITA *(softly)* Thank you.
(*A pause.* DORA *moves below* RITA *to D.L.C.*)
DORA He didn't do it, you know.

RITA H'm?
DORA My husband. He didn't do it.
RITA He told you that?
DORA Yes.
RITA And you believe him?
DORA Of course I believe him! If he'd done it, I'd know all right.
RITA Would you? Yes, I suppose you would. (*Pause.*) The—the police were asking me questions—quite a lot of questions. Some of them—I'm sorry—some of them about your husband.
DORA Yes, I expect they were.
RITA Do they—forgive me asking—do *they* believe he didn't do it?
DORA I dunno what they believe. But I *know* he didn't!
RITA It's nice to be so sure.
DORA Look! If you think Henry did it, why did you come here?
RITA I didn't say I thought——
DORA No, you didn't say it! But it's what you think, isn't it? What were you going to do if you'd come face to face with him, eh? What were you going to do? You'd better get out of here! You shouldn't have come here in the first place! (*A pause. Then more quietly.*) I'm sorry. I shouldn't go on like that, I know. But, you see—he's my husband, and I love him. And nobody's going to hurt him. Not if I can help it.
(*A pause.* RITA *rises to put her cup down on the table.*)
RITA (*gently*) Can he prove he didn't do it?
DORA I'm not sure. That's just the trouble. I'm not sure if he can.
(RITA *moves back to her seat.*)
RITA My husband *was* here last night, wasn't he?
DORA Yes. Yes, he was here. He came to see Henry.
RITA What about?
DORA He wanted him to—to do something for him. (*Suddenly.*) Did you know your husband was going to die?
(*For a moment it seems almost as if* RITA *will begin to cry, but she controls herself.*)
RITA How could I possibly have known that?
DORA Oh, I don't mean last night. I mean—in about six months' time.
RITA I—I don't understand.
DORA He said he was suffering from heart trouble.

E

(RITA *gives a sad smile.*)
RITA So *that's* what he told you?
DORA (*moving to L. of the sofa*) Wasn't it true?
RITA No. Of course it wasn't true! Jimmy was as strong as an ox. He never had a day's illness in his life.
DORA But he told Henry——
RITA Yes. I'm sure he did. (*Still on the verge of tears.*) In the last few years he's—said a lot of things that bore no relation to the truth. I suppose you've never met anyone like that? You're lucky. (*Pause.*) He used to imagine himself in all kinds of dramatic situations that didn't exist at all. And sometimes he would go off into the most terrible rages. Oh, they never lasted long—but it wasn't a very easy thing to live with. (*There is quite a pause.*) What else did he tell your husband?
DORA He offered him money. Three thousand pounds.
RITA And I suppose he wanted to be murdered in return?
(DORA *moves closer to* RITA, *bewildered.*)
DORA How—how did you know?
RITA Oh, it wasn't the first time. That was one of his favourites. I think he enjoyed that one more than any of the others. It gave him a—well, a sense of power, I suppose. And maybe even a bit of excitement. Poor Jimmy. (*She fights back the tears again.*) Most people dismissed it as the make-believe that it was. (*She looks up at* DORA.) But your husband believed him?
DORA (*flatly*) Yes. I suppose so. (*She moves away to the fireplace.*)
RITA And later on he—he came to see Jimmy.
DORA Yes.
RITA I heard them talking in the study.
DORA (*softly*) He didn't do it—
RITA The police were taking fingerprints this morning.
DORA (*firmer*) He didn't do it.
RITA But they don't believe him, do they?
DORA No! No, they don't believe him!
(*The door opens and* THATCHER *comes in. He is carrying his attaché case again. He sees* RITA *as he moves to above the table.*)
THATCHER Mrs. Franklyn. I didn't expect to see you here.
RITA No. I'm sure you didn't, sergeant.
(HENRY *comes in and moves down to* DORA, *who embraces*

SCENE II MURDER FOR THE ASKING

him. *As this happens* THATCHER *puts his case on the chair above the table.*)
HENRY What's *she* doing here?
DORA I don't know, Henry. Oh, thank God you've come back. I've been so frightened
HENRY (*comforting her*) There, there! It'll be all right, luv. You see.
THATCHER I was on my way to see you, Mrs. Franklyn, as a matter of fact.
RITA Then I've saved you a journey, sergeant.
THATCHER I know this is all very distressing for you, but I'm afraid I shall have to ask you a few more questions. (*Moving above the sofa, looking at* HENRY.) It's a matter of confirming or denying other people's evidence.
(HENRY *moves below* DORA *to put his raincoat on the chair* D.L.)
DORA That man was here, Henry. He was in the flat when you left. I was so frightened.
THATCHER (*moving to her*) Mr. Pender?
DORA Yes. He was here. I—I fainted, I'm afraid, and when I came to he'd gone.
THATCHER Not very far, though, Mrs. Scrubb. Only into the arms of the constable on the door.
DORA You mean—you've got him?
THATCHER Er—yes. Been having a very interesting conversation, as a matter of fact.
DORA Then you're not under arrest, Henry?
THATCHER He never was under arrest, Mrs. Scrubb. I told you—there were more questions—you know how it is. (*He turns to* RITA.) Mrs. Franklyn, you told me that you heard Mr. Scrubb visiting your husband last night at about a quarter to ten. That was correct, wasn't it?
RITA Yes. It was about that, I think.
THATCHER And as far as you know there were no other callers between a quarter to ten and the time you found your husband dead?
RITA No.
(THATCHER *crosses below the sofa to the table.*)
THATCHER You told me you were taking a bath at about ten minutes past ten.
RITA That's right.

THATCHER Splashing about a bit, you might not have heard the front door-bell go?
RITA Quite possibly.
THATCHER So somebody could have rung the front door-bell about ten-fifteen and got no answer—so far as you're concerned?
RITA If they did, then I didn't hear it.
THATCHER You came down from your bath about twenty-five minutes past ten.
RITA Yes. (*Pause.*) Jimmy was dead.
(*There is a slight pause.*)
THATCHER Are you sure?
RITA What did you say?
THATCHER I said, are you sure?
RITA Of course I'm sure! Do you think I can forget a thing like that? Do you think I can stop remembering?
THATCHER He was still alive, wasn't he?
(*There is a long pause.* DORA *and* HENRY *do not understand.* RITA *looks at* THATCHER.)
RITA (*softly*) What do you mean?
THATCHER He was still alive when you came down from your bath. You were wearing a blue dressing-gown. He was in his shirt sleeves, just as we found him. But he was alive.
RITA I don't know what you mean. I told you how I found him——
THATCHER It wasn't true, though, was it? I know it wasn't. You see, there was a man outside in the garden, watching you through the window. A man named Fred Pender.
DORA (*looking quickly at* HENRY) Pender?
THATCHER He had an appointment with your husband, but got no answer when he rang the bell. Maybe your husband was on the telephone or something. So he went round to the back of the house to see if anyone was in. And there he saw you.
RITA No, no—it isn't true——!
THATCHER There was a bit of a row going on, wasn't there? Your husband was shouting—getting rather violent——
RITA You must listen to me!
THATCHER You were frightened, weren't you, Mrs. Franklyn? He wouldn't stop shouting at you—over and over again—and you couldn't stand it any longer. So you grabbed up the paper knife from the desk——
RITA It's not true, I tell you—it's not true!

SCENE II MURDER FOR THE ASKING 69

THATCHER —and in a few seconds it was all over!
RITA No! That isn't what happened!
THATCHER It was you, wasn't it? You killed your husband!
RITA (*crying bitterly*) It's not true—it's not true—
(THATCHER *waits for a moment, then moves to the door.*)
THATCHER There's a car outside.
(RITA *rises slowly, collects her handbag and goes slowly out.* THATCHER *prepares to leave. He looks at* HENRY.)
Well—(*Pause.*)—thank you, sir.
HENRY What for?
THATCHER Your co-operation.
(*The two men look at each other for a moment, then* HENRY *turns away, his back to* THATCHER. THATCHER *turns on his heel and walks straight out, closing the door behind him. There is a moment of absolute stillness after he has gone. They listen until the front door is heard to slam, then* HENRY *relaxes.*)
HENRY Well! Thank God for that.
DORA H'm?
HENRY It's all over.
DORA Yes. Yes, I suppose so.
HENRY Well, cheer up, for heaven's sake! We've got something to celebrate. (*He moves away below the sofa.*)
DORA Yes—I'm sorry, Henry. (*She sits in the armchair, subdued.*)
HENRY What's up now?
DORA It's just that—when Fred Pender was here this afternoon, he said that Mr. Franklyn was still alive when he left the house last night.
HENRY What of it?
DORA So he—he *didn't* see how he died.
HENRY What does it matter? *She* didn't know that, did she? Now she'll confess the whole thing. I expect that was the sergeant's little trap. He's always up to something like that.
DORA It just seemed—odd, somehow.
HENRY (*moving to her*) Oh, come off it, Dora! What difference does it make what Pender saw? The sergeant's satisfied. That's all that matters. We can relax now and forget it. Relax and enjoy ourselves.
DORA Relax?
HENRY Well—it's all over now. Everything's all right. From now on we've nothing to worry about.

DORA Haven't we? Our life hasn't changed. Nothing's different for *us*.
(*He turns away from her.*)
HENRY Oh, come on, Dora! Be your age. We're better off.
DORA Yes, better off because you're in the clear now, but——
(*He turns abruptly.*)
HENRY (*fiercely*) Better off by three thousand pounds!
(*There is a pause.* DORA *gazes at him in horror.*)
DORA Henry—what do you mean?
HENRY You didn't *believe* all that stuff about Mrs. Franklyn, did you?
DORA (*rising*) You—you didn't really do it? You didn't kill him?
HENRY Of course I killed him! It was too good to be missed. I was doing him a favour—he *asked* me to do it! He *wanted* me to do it!
DORA (*crying*) Oh, no—no, Henry—you couldn't have—you couldn't have——
HENRY It's all over, Dora. I told you—we're in the clear. The sergeant's satisfied. We're free and in the clear.
DORA But he thinks Mrs. Franklyn did it!
HENRY What of it?
DORA But she didn't!
HENRY So what does it matter, then? They may *charge* her with it, but they'll never be able to prove she's guilty—in the end they'll have to release her. And here we are three thousand pounds better off.
DORA You couldn't have done it—you couldn't have—
(*She is crying as the door opens and* THATCHER *walks back in.*)
THATCHER Sorry to trouble you again, sir, but I left my case behind. (*He goes to his case.*)
HENRY I—I thought you'd gone. We heard the front door go.
THATCHER Like I said, sir—people think I've gone for good, and then suddenly there I am!
(*He looks across at* DORA, *who is attempting to control herself.*)
Is everything all right, Mrs. Scrubb?
DORA (*after looking at* HENRY) Yes. Yes, thank you. (*She subsides into a chair.*)
THATCHER (*putting his case on the table*) She—er—she played her part well, didn't she, sir?

SCENE II MURDER FOR THE ASKING 71

HENRY Eh?
THATCHER Mrs. Franklyn. She put up a good performance.
HENRY I don't know what you mean.
THATCHER Didn't it ever strike you as peculiar that Mrs. Franklyn should call here? I mean, how did she know the address? *(Pause.)* Because I told her. I *asked* her to come. And I told her the little charade I wanted her to play with me.
HENRY You mean—it wasn't true?
THATCHER Not the bit about how he died. We made that up between us.
HENRY Why? Why should you do that?
THATCHER Once you thought you were in the clear I reckoned you'd give yourself away. And I was right, wasn't I? Mind you, it did happen a lot quicker than I expected.
HENRY I—I don't know what you're talking about.
(THATCHER *opens his attaché case and turns a switch on the tape recorder inside. We hear the recorded voices of* DORA *and* HENRY.)
HENRY *(on tape)* 'Henry—what do you mean?'
DORA *(on tape)* 'You didn't *believe* all that stuff about Mrs. Franklyn, did you?'
DORA *(on tape)* 'You—you didn't really do it? You didn't kill him?'
HENRY *(on tape)* 'Of course I killed him! It was too good to be missed. I was doing him a favour—he *asked* me to do it! He *wanted* me to do it!'
(THATCHER *switches off the machine and closes the case.*)
HENRY You'll never be able to use that!
THATCHER *(facing him, grimly)* You want a bet?
HENRY So—after you'd gone out of here—if I'd kept my mouth shut—if I'd never said a word——?
THATCHER Then we'd probably never have known, would we?
(THATCHER *collects his hat and case and turns again to* HENRY.)
How did you think you were going to collect? Where did Franklyn tell you he'd put it? A left luggage office, something like that?
(HENRY *looks at him, but makes no reply.*)
It wouldn't have been there, you know—because there never was any money. So you'd have done it all for nothing.

THATCHER *moves to the door and opens it. He looks back at* HENRY, *waiting.* HENRY *moves slowly towards* DORA *and looks at her helplessly. She backs away from him, trembling with shock. He starts to move slowly towards the door as—*

THE CURTAIN FALLS

PROPERTY PLOT

ACT I

SCENE 1

Set:
    Newspaper (*on floor*. HENRY)
    Carrier bag containing groceries (*off* R. DORA)
    Paper bag containing jumper (*off* R. DORA)
    Handbag (*off* R. DORA)
    Two evening papers (*off* R. DORA)
    Key (*mantelpiece*. DORA)
    Tablecloth (*kitchenette drawer*. DORA)
    Henry's tie (*off* L. HENRY)
    Henry's jacket (*chair*. HENRY)
    Bottle of beer (*kitchenette*. HENRY)
    Glass (*kitchenette*. HENRY)
    Matches (*mantelpiece*)
    Matches (*sideboard*)
    Ashtray (*mantelpiece*)
    Ashtray (*table* R.)
    Newspapers (*under sofa cushions*. HENRY)
    Tea-pot containing tea (*kitchenette*. DORA)
    Three tea-spoons (*kitchenette*. DORA)
    Tea cosy (*kitchenette*. DORA)
    Plate of cold fish-and-chips (*oven*. DORA)
    Towel (*off* R. HENRY)
    Two plates
    Two cups and saucers
    Sugar bowl with sugar
    Milk jug with milk
    Loaf of bread   (*kitchenette*)
    Bread board
    Bread knife
    Butter dish with butter
    Pot of marmalade

SCENE II

Set:
    Kettle with boiling water (*kitchenette*)
    Henry's shoes (*near the sofa*)
    Henry's jacket (*back of sofa*)
    Newspaper (*on sofa.* HENRY)
    Dora's handbag (*kitchenette*)

ACT II

Set:
    Newspaper (*off* R. JANET)

ACT III

SCENE I

Set:
    Shopping bag of groceries (*off* R. DORA)
    Attaché case containing silver articles (*off* R. THATCHER)
    Identical attaché case containing tape recorder (*off* R. THATCHER)

SCENE II

Set:
    One cup and saucer with tea (DORA)
    Two cups and saucers ⎫
    Tea-pot containing tea ⎪
    Milk jug with milk ⎬   (*Table* R.)
    Sugar bowl with sugar ⎭

Personal:
FRANKLYN
    Cigars in case
    List of names
    Visiting card

PROPERTY PLOT

THATCHER
   Identification card
   Letter
   Packet of cigarettes
   Cigarette lighter

HENRY
   List of names

PENDER
   Cigarette

RITA
   Handkerchief

Effects:
   Radio playing
   Door-bell
   Door slam
   Practical tape recorder

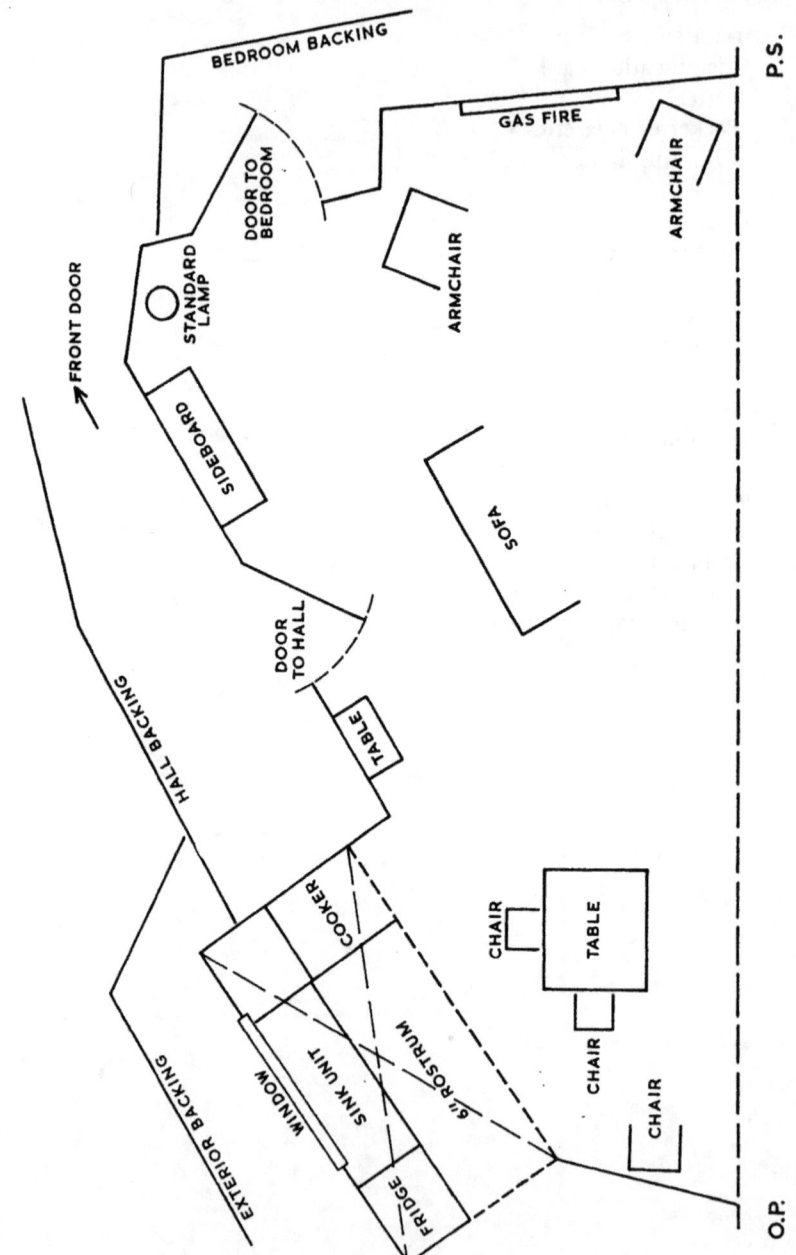

PRODUCTION NOTE

'Murder for the Asking' is, of course, primarily a mystery play. Perhaps not so much a 'who-dun-it' as a 'did-he-do-it?' The play begins in an ordinary, everyday way but we are soon aware that there is something odd going on. Why is Henry so keen to get Dora out of the house? We feel that he is up to something. Then, with the taking of Dora's key, we are sure of it and in no time at all we are meeting Mr. Franklyn and hearing of his strange request. From then on our interest is in Henry's reactions to the situation. During the end of Act One and the early part of Act Two the audience's feelings are mixed and confused. Did he do it? Or didn't he? If he did do it, is he going to get away with it? And if he didn't do it, are the police going to get him for it, anyway? By the end of the second Act, however, there is no doubt in our minds. We are absolutely convinced of Henry's innocence; and from then on we are worried, as he is, whether he will ever be able to explain away his actions and reactions sufficiently to clear himself.

As I said, this is a mystery play and there is no doubt that the final twist at the end really takes the audience by surprise, but I hope it is also a play about people. I have tried to write about real people to whom unexpected things happen, and whose lives are changed through circumstances and ill luck. I have tried to make the characters interesting as characters and not just as cogs in the wheels of the plot. The relationship between Henry and Dora forms the foundation of the whole play and this must be established clearly in the opening scene. We must care about them, and worry about them, and then our horror at the final dénouement will be the greater.

Above all things, Henry must have a sympathetic personality. He is weak. He is lazy. But he is likeable. Dora is the dominant one of the partnership. Without her, Henry would be lost. It is she who constantly fights to keep them out of financial trouble. Henry is the born failure. Whatever he tries his hand at he always seems to fall short, and it is Dora who props him up, collects up the pieces and urges him to try again. When in Act One, Scene One, he says, 'There's only one thing for us to do. Move away from here. Start afresh—you know', we must know from Dora's reaction that this is the old routine, and though she knows that wherever they went things would never be different she loves him enough not to tell him that the fault is not in places or circumstances but in himself.

The relationship between Henry and Thatcher should also be such that their scenes become not only the question-and-answer of police interrogation but also the clash of two personalities. Thatcher is ambitious, ruthless and determined. In Henry he sees a man who is vulnerable and he sets upon this and attacks his weaknesses at every point. Thatcher enjoys the game of cut-and-thrust, and the scenes between the two can be fascinating as the advantage sways this way and that. There is quite a lot of comedy to be had out of Thatcher, and this does not in any way detract from the drama of the situation. It does, in fact, heighten it and his varying moods of flippancy and sudden attack make him more rewarding to play and more interesting to watch.

The real character of Franklyn is only revealed in Act Three, Scene Two, and in Franklyn's own scene at the beginning of the play it is essential that we believe him to be sincere in his request and that we accept his reasons for making it. We will find him strange and awe-inspiring, as Henry does, and feel that there is something almost frightening about the atmosphere he generates. But it must be an atmosphere generated of itself and not by theatrical over-emphasis. We must never think him to be mad. His request is unprecedented, but it is essential for the play that we believe he is sincere in making it.

The other characters are clearly defined—Rita Franklyn, sad-eyed and gentle; Janet Gregory, a cheerful Cockney who provides plenty of comic relief; and Fred Pender, a rough-looking man whom we and Dora are prepared to believe may be a murderer.

It is important not to cheat and overdo the playing of Pender in an attempt to heighten the drama. He is merely a man who comes in response to a message, thinking there may be money in it for him. He knows nothing of murder until Dora tells him and then he is frightened of getting involved, and it is for this reason only that he tries to stop Dora going for the police. The plot of the play has led us to believe that he may be a murderer, so play the part only for what he *is* and our imagination (and Dora's) will do the rest.

A word about the setting. It need not be drab. Though Henry has been having a bad time, Dora is in work and she is the type of woman who would have taken pride in her home, however humble, and would certainly have brightened it up with pleasant curtains, cushion covers, etc. It is a furnished flat, so the furniture need not be

PRODUCTION NOTE

a reflection of Henry's financial position. The lighting, too, can help to make the set interesting to look at as well as contributing to the general atmosphere.

One technical point: it is essential in Act Three that the attaché cases used by Thatcher are identical. This will ensure that we do not suspect the presence of a tape recorder at the end. As marked on page 67 Thatcher should put down the attaché case on the chair above the table during the distraction of Henry crossing and meeting Dora. On the table should be a chenille cloth which will conceal the case from our view. It would be a pity if, on Thatcher's exit after Rita Franklyn, we saw that he had left his case and therefore knew that he would have to return. The tape recorder in the case is practical, but it is advisable to have a stand-by recording at the ready in the wings in case of accident.

D.B.

www.ingramcontent.com/pod-product-compliance
Lightning Source LLC
LaVergne TN
LVHW051759080426
835511LV00018B/3358